Introducing Regular Expressions

Michael Fitzgerald

O'REILLY®

Beijing · Cambridge · Farnham · Köln · Sebastopol · Tokyo

Introducing Regular Expressions

by Michael Fitzgerald

Published by O'Reilly Media, Inc., 1005 Gravenstein Highway North, Sebastopol, CA 95472.

O'Reilly books may be purchased for educational, business, or sales promotional use. Online editions are also available for most titles (*http://my.safaribooksonline.com*). For more information, contact our corporate/institutional sales department: 800-998-9938 or *corporate@oreilly.com*.

Editor: Simon St. Laurent
Production Editor: Holly Bauer

Proofreader: Julie Van Keuren
Indexer: Lucie Haskins
Cover Designer: Karen Montgomery
Interior Designer: David Futato
Illustrator: Rebecca Demarest

July 2012:   First Edition

Revision History for the First Edition:

2012-07-10   First release

2012-12-12   Second release

See *http://oreilly.com/catalog/errata.csp?isbn=9781449392680* for release details.

ISBN: 978-1-449-39268-0

[LSI]

Table of Contents

Preface

This book shows you how to write regular expressions through examples. Its goal is to make learning regular expressions as easy as possible. In fact, this book demonstrates nearly every concept it presents by way of example so you can easily imitate and try them yourself.

Regular expressions help you find patterns in text strings. More precisely, they are specially encoded text strings that match patterns in sets of strings, most often strings that are found in documents or files.

Regular expressions began to emerge when mathematician Stephen Kleene wrote his book *Introduction to Metamathematics* (New York, Van Nostrand), first published in 1952, though the concepts had been around since the early 1940s. They became more widely available to computer scientists with the advent of the Unix operating system—the work of Brian Kernighan, Dennis Ritchie, Ken Thompson, and others at AT&T Bell Labs—and its utilities, such as *sed* and *grep*, in the early 1970s.

The earliest appearance that I can find of regular expressions in a computer application is in the QED editor. QED, short for Quick Editor, was written for the Berkeley Time-sharing System, which ran on the Scientific Data Systems SDS 940. Documented in 1970, it was a rewrite by Ken Thompson of a previous editor on MIT's Compatible Time-Sharing System and yielded one of the earliest if not first practical implementations of regular expressions in computing. (Table A-1 in Appendix A documents the regex features of QED.)

I'll use a variety of tools to demonstrate the examples. You will, I hope, find most of them usable and useful; others won't be usable because they are not readily available on your Windows system. You can skip the ones that aren't practical for you or that aren't appealing. But I recommend that anyone who is serious about a career in computing learn about regular expressions in a Unix-based environment. I have worked in that environment for 25 years and still learn new things every day.

> "Those who don't understand Unix are condemned to reinvent it, poorly." —Henry Spencer

Some of the tools I'll show you are available online via a web browser, which will be the easiest for most readers to use. Others you'll use from a command or a shell prompt, and a few you'll run on the desktop. The tools, if you don't have them, will be easy to download. The majority are free or won't cost you much money.

This book also goes light on jargon. I'll share with you what the correct terms are when necessary, but in small doses. I use this approach because over the years, I've found that jargon can often create barriers. In other words, I'll try not to overwhelm you with the dry language that describes regular expressions. That is because the basic philosophy of this book is this: Doing useful things can come before knowing everything about a given subject.

There are lots of different implementations of regular expressions. You will find regular expressions used in Unix command-line tools like *vi* (*vim*), *grep*, and *sed*, among others. You will find regular expressions in programming languages like Perl (of course), Java, JavaScript, C# or Ruby, and many more, and you will find them in declarative languages like XSLT 2.0. You will also find them in applications like Notepad++, Oxygen, or TextMate, among many others.

Most of these implementations have similarities and differences. I won't cover all those differences in this book, but I will touch on a good number of them. If I attempted to document *all* the differences between *all* implementations, I'd have to be hospitalized. I won't get bogged down in these kinds of details in this book. You're expecting an introductory text, as advertised, and that is what you'll get.

Who Should Read This Book

The audience for this book is people who haven't ever written a regular expression before. If you are new to regular expressions or programming, this book is a good place to start. In other words, I am writing for the reader who has heard of regular expressions and is interested in them but who doesn't really understand them yet. If that is you, then this book is a good fit.

The order I'll go in to cover the features of regex is from the simple to the complex. In other words, we'll go step by simple step.

Now, if you happen to already know something about regular expressions and how to use them, or if you are an experienced programmer, this book may not be where you want to start. This is a beginner's book, for rank beginners who need some hand-holding. If you have written some regular expressions before, and feel familiar with them, you can start here if you want, but I'm planning to take it slower than you will probably like.

I recommend several books to read after this one. First, try Jeff Friedl's *Mastering Regular Expressions, Third Edition* (see *http://shop.oreilly.com/product/9781565922570.do*). Friedl's book gives regular expressions a thorough going over, and I highly recommend it. I also recommend the *Regular Expressions Cookbook* (see *http://shop.oreilly.com/product/9780596520694.do*) by Jan Goyvaerts and Steven Levithan. Jan Goyvaerts is the creator of RegexBuddy, a powerful desktop application (see *http://www.regexbuddy.com/*). Steven Levithan created RegexPal, an online regular expression processor that you'll use in the first chapter of this book (see *http://www.regexpal.com*).

What You Need to Use This Book

To get the most out of this book, you'll need access to tools available on Unix or Linux operating systems, such as Darwin on the Mac, a variant of BSD (Berkeley Software Distribution) on the Mac, or Cygwin on a Windows PC, which offers many GNU tools in its distribution (see *http://www.cygwin.com* and *http://www.gnu.org*).

There will be plenty of examples for you to try out here. You can just read them if you want, but to really learn, you'll need to follow as many of them as you can, as the most important kind of learning, I think, always comes from doing, not from standing on the sidelines. You'll be introduced to websites that will teach you what regular expressions are by highlighting matched results, workhorse command line tools from the Unix world, and desktop applications that analyze regular expressions or use them to perform text search.

You will find examples from this book on Github at *https://github.com/michaeljames fitzgerald/Introducing-Regular-Expressions*. You will also find an archive of all the examples and test files in this book for download from *http://examples.oreilly.com/0636920012337/examples.zip*. It would be best if you create a working directory or folder on your computer and then download these files to that directory before you dive into the book.

Conventions Used in This Book

The following typographical conventions are used in this book:

Italic
> Indicates new terms, URLs, email addresses, filenames, file extensions, and so forth.

`Constant width`

Used for program listings, as well as within paragraphs, to refer to program elements such as expressions and command lines or any other programmatic elements.

 This icon signifies a tip, suggestion, or a general note.

Using Code Examples

This book is here to help you get your job done. In general, you may use the code in this book in your programs and documentation. You do not need to contact us for permission unless you're reproducing a significant portion of the code. For example, writing a program that uses several chunks of code from this book does not require permission. Selling or distributing a CD-ROM of examples from O'Reilly books does require permission. Answering a question by citing this book and quoting example code does not require permission. Incorporating a significant amount of example code from this book into your product's documentation does require permission.

We appreciate, but do not require, attribution. An attribution usually includes the title, author, publisher, and ISBN. For example: "*Introducing Regular Expressions* by Michael Fitzgerald (O'Reilly). Copyright 2012 Michael Fitzgerald, 978-1-4493-9268-0."

If you feel your use of code examples falls outside fair use or the permission given above, feel free to contact O'Reilly at *permissions@oreilly.com*.

Safari® Books Online

 Safari Books Online (www.safaribooksonline.com (*http://my.safari booksonline.com/?portal=oreilly*)) is an on-demand digital library that delivers expert content (*http://www.safaribooksonline.com/content*) in both book and video form from the world's leading authors in technology and business.

Technology professionals, software developers, web designers, and business and creative professionals use Safari Books Online as their primary resource for research, problem solving, learning, and certification training.

Safari Books Online offers a range of product mixes (*http://www.safaribooksonline.com/ subscriptions*) and pricing programs for organizations (*http://www.safaribookson line.com/organizations-teams*), government agencies (*http://www.safaribookson line.com/government*), and individuals (*http://www.safaribooksonline.com/individuals*).

Subscribers have access to thousands of books, training videos, and prepublication manuscripts in one fully searchable database from publishers like O'Reilly Media, Prentice Hall Professional, Addison-Wesley Professional, Microsoft Press, Sams, Que, Peachpit Press, Focal Press, Cisco Press, John Wiley & Sons, Syngress, Morgan Kaufmann, IBM Redbooks, Packt, Adobe Press, FT Press, Apress, Manning, New Riders, McGraw-Hill, Jones & Bartlett, Course Technology, and dozens more (*http://www.safaribookson line.com/publishers*). For more information about Safari Books Online, please visit us online (*http://www.safaribooksonline.com/*).

How to Contact Us

Please address comments and questions concerning this book to the publisher:

O'Reilly Media, Inc. 1005 Gravenstein Highway North Sebastopol, CA 95472 800-998-9938 (in the United States or Canada) 707-829-0515 (international or local) 707-829-0104 (fax)

This book has a web page listing errata, examples, and any additional information. You can access this page at:

http://oreil.ly/intro_regex

To comment or to ask technical questions about this book, send email to:

bookquestions@oreilly.com

For more information about O'Reilly books, courses, conferences, and news, see its website at *http://www.oreilly.com*.

Find O'Reilly on Facebook: *http://facebook.com/oreilly*

Follow O'Reilly on Twitter: *http://twitter.com/oreillymedia*

Watch O'Reilly on YouTube: *http://www.youtube.com/oreillymedia*

Acknowledgments

Once again, I want to express appreciation to my editor at O'Reilly, Simon St. Laurent, a very patient man without whom this book would never have seen the light of day. Thank you to Seara Patterson Coburn and Roger Zauner for your helpful reviews. And, as always, I want to recognize the love of my life, Cristi, who is my *raison d'être*.

CHAPTER 1

What Is a Regular Expression?

Regular expressions are specially encoded text strings used as patterns for matching sets of strings. They began to emerge in the 1940s as a way to describe regular languages, but they really began to show up in the programming world during the 1970s. The first place I could find them showing up was in the QED text editor written by Ken Thompson.

> "A regular expression is a pattern which specifies a set of strings of characters; it is said to match certain strings." —Ken Thompson

Regular expressions later became an important part of the tool suite that emerged from the Unix operating system—the *ed*, *sed* and *vi* (*vim*) editors, *grep*, *AWK*, among others. But the ways in which regular expressions were implemented were not always so regular.

This book takes an inductive approach; in other words, it moves from the specific to the general. So rather than an example after a treatise, you will often get the example first and then a short treatise following that. It's a learn-by-doing book.

Regular expressions have a reputation for being gnarly, but that all depends on how you approach them. There is a natural progression from something as simple as this:

```
\d
```

a *character shorthand* that matches any digit from 0 to 9, to something a bit more complicated, like:

```
^(\(\d{3}\)|^\d{3}[.-]?)?\d{3}[.-]?\d{4}$
```

which is where we'll wind up at the end of this chapter: a fairly robust regular expression that matches a 10-digit, North American telephone number, with or without parentheses around the area code, or with or without hyphens or dots (periods) to separate the numbers. (The parentheses must be balanced, too; in other words, you can't just have one.)

Chapter 10 shows you a slightly more sophisticated regular expression for a phone number, but the one above is sufficient for the purposes of this chapter.

If you don't get how that all works yet, don't worry: I'll explain the whole expression a little at a time in this chapter. If you will just follow the examples (and those throughout the book, for that matter), writing regular expressions will soon become second nature to you. Ready to find out for yourself?

I at times represent Unicode characters in this book using their code point—a four-digit, hexadecimal (base 16) number. These code points are shown in the form *U+0000*. U+002E, for example, represents the code point for a full stop or period (.).

Getting Started with Regexpal

First let me introduce you to the Regexpal website at *http://www.regexpal.com*. Open the site up in a browser, such as Google Chrome or Mozilla Firefox. You can see what the site looks like in Figure 1-1.

You can see that there is a text area near the top, and a larger text area below that. The top text box is for entering regular expressions, and the bottom one holds the subject or target text. The target text is the text or set of strings that you want to match.

At the end of this chapter and each following chapter, you'll find a "Technical Notes" section. These notes provide additional information about the technology discussed in the chapter and tell you where to get more information about that technology. Placing these notes at the end of the chapters helps keep the flow of the main text moving forward rather than stopping to discuss each detail along the way.

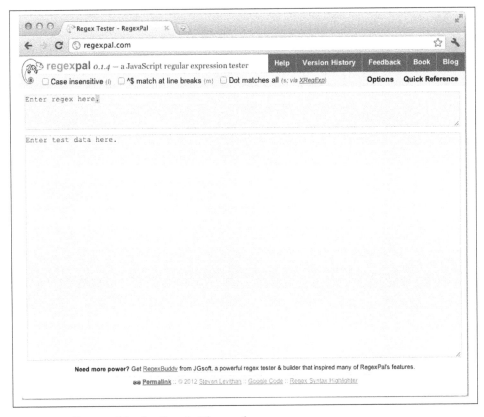

Figure 1-1. Regexpal in the Google Chrome browser

Matching a North American Phone Number

Now we'll match a North American phone number with a regular expression. Type the phone number shown here into the lower section of Regexpal:

    707-827-7019

Do you recognize it? It's the number for O'Reilly Media.

Let's match that number with a regular expression. There are lots of ways to do this, but to start out, simply enter the number itself in the upper section, exactly as it is written in the lower section (hold on now, don't sigh):

    707-827-7019

What you should see is the phone number you entered in the lower box highlighted from beginning to end in yellow. If that is what you see (as shown in Figure 1-2), then you are in business.

When I mention colors in this book, in relation to something you might see in an image or a screenshot, such as the highlighting in Regexpal, those colors may appear online and in e-book versions of this book, but, alas, not in print. So if you are reading this book on paper, then when I mention a color, your world will be grayscale, with my apologies.

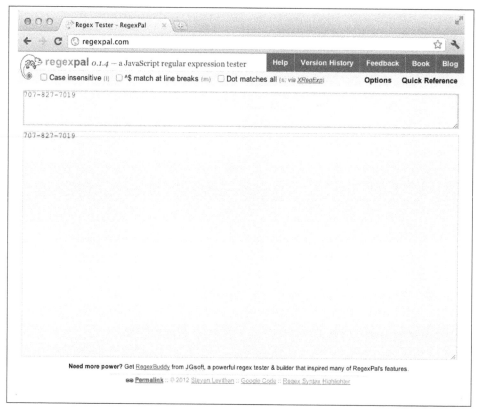

Figure 1-2. Ten-digit phone number highlighted in Regexpal

What you have done in this regular expression is use something called a *string literal* to match a string in the target text. A string literal is a literal representation of a string.

Now delete the number in the upper box and replace it with just the number 7. Did you see what happened? Now only the sevens are highlighted. The literal character (number) 7 in the regular expression matches the four instances of the number 7 in the text you are matching.

Matching Digits with a Character Class

What if you wanted to match all the numbers in the phone number, all at once? Or match any number for that matter?

Try the following, exactly as shown, once again in the upper text box:

```
[0-9]
```

All the numbers (more precisely *digits*) in the lower section are highlighted, in alternating yellow and blue. What the regular expression \[0-9\] is saying to the regex processor is, "Match any digit you find in the range 0 through 9."

The square brackets are not literally matched because they are treated specially as *metacharacters*. A metacharacter has special meaning in regular expressions and is reserved. A regular expression in the form \[0-9\] is called a *character class*, or sometimes a *character set*.

You can limit the range of digits more precisely and get the same result using a more specific list of digits to match, such as the following:

```
[012789]
```

This will match only those digits listed, that is, 0, 1, 2, 7, 8, and 9. Try it in the upper box. Once again, every digit in the lower box will be highlighted in alternating colors.

To match any 10-digit, North American phone number, whose parts are separated by hyphens, you could do the following:

```
[0-9][0-9][0-9]-[0-9][0-9][0-9]-[0-9][0-9][0-9][0-9]
```

This will work, but it's bombastic. There is a better way with something called a shorthand.

Using a Character Shorthand

Yet another way to match digits, which you saw at the beginning of the chapter, is with \d which, by itself, will match all Arabic digits, just like \[0-9\]. Try that in the top section and, as with the previous regular expressions, the digits below will be highlighted. This kind of regular expression is called a *character shorthand*. (It is also called a *character escape*, but this term can be a little misleading, so I avoid it. I'll explain later.)

To match any digit in the phone number, you could also do this:

```
\d\d\d-\d\d\d-\d\d\d\d
```

Repeating the \d three and four times in sequence will exactly match three and four digits in sequence. The hyphen in the above regular expression is entered as a literal character and will be matched as such.

What about those hyphens? How do you match them? You can use a literal hyphen (-) as already shown, or you could use an escaped uppercase *D* (\D), which matches any character that is *not* a digit.

This sample uses \D in place of the literal hyphen:

```
\d\d\d\D\d\d\d\D\d\d\d\d
```

Once again, the entire phone number, including the hyphens, should be highlighted this time.

Matching Any Character

You could also match those pesky hyphens with a dot (.):

```
\d\d\d.\d\d\d.\d\d\d\d
```

The dot or period essentially acts as a wildcard and will match any character (except, in certain situations, a line ending). In the example above, the regular expression matches the hyphen, but it could also match a percent sign (%):

```
707%827%7019
```

Or a vertical bar (|):

```
707|827|7019
```

Or any other character.

 As I mentioned, the dot character (officially, the full stop) will not normally match a new line character, such as a line feed (U+000A). However, there are ways to make it possible to match a newline with a dot, which I will show you later. This is often called the *dotall* option.

Capturing Groups and Back References

You'll now match just a portion of the phone number using what is known as a *capturing group*. Then you'll refer to the content of the group with a *backreference*. To create a capturing group, enclose a \d in a pair of parentheses to place it in a group, and then follow it with a \1 to backreference what was captured:

```
(\d)\d\1
```

The \1 refers back to what was captured in the group enclosed by parentheses. As a result, this regular expression matches the prefix 707. Here is a breakdown of it:

- (\d) matches the first digit and captures it (the number *7*)
- \d matches the next digit (the number *0*) but does not capture it because it is not enclosed in parentheses
- \1 references the captured digit (the number *7*)

This will match only the area code. Don't worry if you don't fully understand this right now. You'll see plenty of examples of groups later in the book.

You could now match the whole phone number with one group and several backreferences:

```
(\d)0\1\D\d\d\1\D\1\d\d\d
```

But that's not quite as elegant as it could be. Let's try something that works even better.

Using Quantifiers

Here is yet another way to match a phone number using a different syntax:

```
\d{3}-?\d{3}-?\d{4}
```

The numbers in the curly braces tell the regex processor *exactly* how many occurrences of those digits you want it to look for. The braces with numbers are a kind of *quantifier*. The braces themselves are considered metacharacters.

The question mark (?) is another kind of quantifier. It follows the hyphen in the regular expression above and means that the hyphen is optional—that is, that there can be zero or one occurrence of the hyphen (one or none). There are other quantifiers such as the plus sign (+), which means "one or more," or the asterisk (*) which means "zero or more."

Using quantifiers, you can make a regular expression even more concise:

```
(\d{3,4}[.-]?)+
```

The plus sign again means that the quantity can occur one or more times. This regular expression will match either three or four digits, followed by an optional hyphen or dot, grouped together by parentheses, one or more times (+).

Is your head spinning? I hope not. Here's a character-by-character analysis of the regular expression above:

- (open a capturing group
- \ start character shorthand (escape the following character)

- d end character shorthand (match any digit in the range 0 through 9 with \d)
- { open quantifier
- 3 minimum quantity to match
- , separate quantities
- 4 maximum quantity to match
- } close quantifier
- \[open character class
- . dot or period (matches literal dot)
- - literal character to match hyphen
- \] close character class
- ? zero or one quantifier
-) close capturing group
- + one or more quantifier

This all works, but it's not quite right because it will also match other groups of 3 or 4 digits, whether in the form of a phone number or not. Yes, we learn from our mistakes better than our successes.

So let's improve it a little:

```
(\d{3}[.-]?){2}\d{4}
```

This will match two nonparenthesized sequences of three digits each, followed by an optional hyphen, and then followed by exactly four digits.

Quoting Literals

Finally, here is a regular expression that allows literal parentheses to optionally wrap the first sequence of three digits, and makes the area code optional as well:

```
^(\(\d{3}\)|^\d{3}[.-]?)?\d{3}[.-]?\d{4}$
```

To ensure that it is easy to decipher, I'll look at this one character by character, too:

- \^ (caret) at the beginning of the regular expression, or following the vertical bar (|), means that the phone number will be at the beginning of a line.
- (opens a capturing group.
- \(is a literal open parenthesis.
- \d matches a digit.
- {3} is a quantifier that, following \d, matches exactly three digits.

- \) matches a literal close parenthesis.
- | (the vertical bar) indicates *alternation*, that is, a given choice of alternatives. In other words, this says "match an area code with parentheses or without them."
- \^ matches the beginning of a line.
- \d matches a digit.
- {3} is a quantifier that matches exactly three digits.
- \[.-\]? matches an optional dot or hyphen.
-) close capturing group.
- ? make the group optional, that is, the prefix in the group is not required.
- \d matches a digit.
- {3} matches exactly three digits.
- \[.-\]? matches another optional dot or hyphen.
- \d matches a digit.
- {4} matches exactly four digits.
- $ matches the end of a line.

This final regular expression matches a 10-digit, North American telephone number, with or without parentheses, hyphens, or dots. Try different forms of the number to see what will match (and what won't).

The capturing group in the above regular expression is not necessary. The group is necessary, but the capturing part is not. There is a better way to do this: a non-capturing group. When we revisit this regular expression in the last chapter of the book, you'll understand why.

A Sample of Applications

To conclude this chapter, I'll show you the regular expression for a phone number in several applications.

TextMate is an editor that is available only on the Mac and uses the same regular expression library as the Ruby programming language. You can use regular expressions through the Find (search) feature, as shown in Figure 1-3. Check the box next to *Regular expression*.

Notepad++ is available on Windows and is a popular, free editor that uses the PCRE regular expression library. You can access them through search and replace (Figure 1-4) by clicking the radio button next to *Regular expression*.

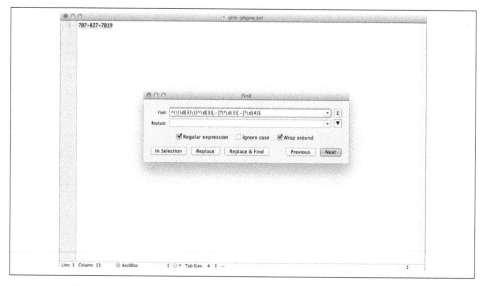

Figure 1-3. Phone number regex in TextMate

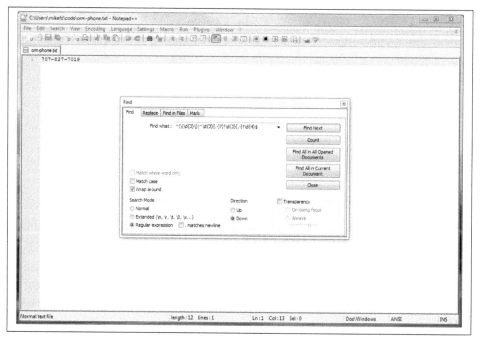

Figure 1-4. Phone number regex in Notepad++

Oxygen is also a popular and powerful XML editor that uses Perl 5 regular expression syntax. You can access regular expressions through the search and replace dialog, as shown in Figure 1-5, or through its regular expression builder for XML Schema. To use regular expressions with Find/Replace, check the box next to *Regular expression*.

Figure 1-5. Phone number regex in Oxygen

This is where the introduction ends. Congratulations. You've covered a lot of ground in this chapter. In the next chapter, we'll focus on simple pattern matching.

What You Learned in Chapter 1

- What a regular expression is
- How to use Regexpal, a simple regular expression processor
- How to match string literals
- How to match digits with a character class
- How to match a digit with a character shorthand
- How to match a non-digit with a character shorthand
- How to use a capturing group and a backreference
- How to match an exact quantity of a set of strings

- How to match a character optionally (zero or one) or one or more times
- How to match strings at either the beginning or the end of a line

Technical Notes

- Regexpal (*http://www.regexpal.com*) is a web-based, JavaScript-powered regex implementation. It's not the most complete implementation, and it doesn't do everything that regular expressions can do; however, it's a clean, simple, and very easy-to-use learning tool, and it provides plenty of features for you to get started.

- You can download the Chrome browser from *https://www.google.com/chrome* or Firefox from *http://www.mozilla.org/en-US/firefox/new/*.

- Why are there so many ways of doing things with regular expressions? One reason is because regular expressions have a wonderful quality called *composability*. A language, whether a formal, programming or schema language, that has the quality of *composability* (James Clark explains it well at *http://www.thaiopensource.com/relaxng/design.html#section:5*) is one that lets you take its atomic parts and composition methods and then recombine them easily in different ways. Once you learn the different parts of regular expressions, you will take off in your ability to match strings of any kind.

- TextMate is available at *http://www.macromates.com*. For more information on regular expressions in TextMate, see *http://manual.macromates.com/en/regular_expressions*.

- For more information on Notepad, see *http://notepad-plus-plus.org*. For documentation on using regular expressions with Notepad, see *http://sourceforge.net/apps/mediawiki/notepad-plus/index.php?title=Regular_Expressions*.

- Find out more about Oxygen at *http://www.oxygenxml.com*. For information on using regex through find and replace, see *http://www.oxygenxml.com/doc/ug-editor/topics/find-replace-dialog.html*. For information on using its regular expression builder for XML Schema, see *http://www.oxygenxml.com/doc/ug-editor/topics/XML-schema-regexp-builder.html*.

CHAPTER 2

Simple Pattern Matching

Regular expressions are all about matching and finding patterns in text, from simple patterns to the very complex. This chapter takes you on a tour of some of the simpler ways to match patterns using:

- String literals
- Digits
- Letters
- Characters of any kind

In the first chapter, we used Steven Levithan's RegexPal to demonstrate regular expressions. In this chapter, we'll use Grant Skinner's RegExr site, found at *http://gskinner.com/ regexr* (see Figure 2-1).

 Each page of this book will take you deeper into the regular expression jungle. Feel free, however, to stop and smell the syntax. What I mean is, start trying out new things as soon as you discover them. Try. Fail fast. Get a grip. Move on. Nothing makes learning sink in like *doing* something with it.

Before we go any further, I want to point out the helps that RegExr provides. Over on the right side of RegExr, you'll see three tabs. Take note of the Samples and Community tabs. The Samples tab provides helps for a lot of regular expression syntax, and the Community tab shows you a large number of contributed regular expressions that have been rated. You'll find a lot of good information in these tabs that may be useful to you. In addition, pop-ups appear when you hover over the regular expression or target text in RegExr, giving you helpful information. These resources are one of the reasons why RegExr is among my favorite online regex checkers.

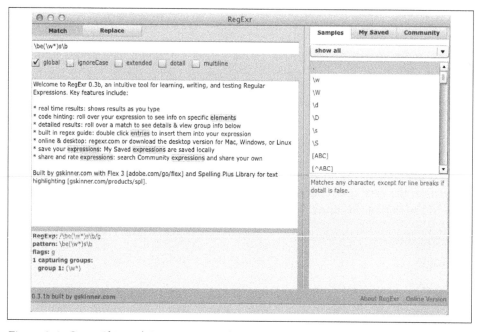

Figure 2-1. Grant Skinner's RegExr in Firefox

This chapter introduces you to our main text, "The Rime of the Ancient Mariner," by Samuel Taylor Coleridge, first published in *Lyrical Ballads* (London, J. & A. Arch, 1798). We'll work with this poem in chapters that follow, starting with a plain-text version of the original and winding up with a version marked up in HTML5. The text for the whole poem is stored in a file called *rime.txt*; this chapter uses the file *rime-intro.txt* that contains only the first few lines.

The following lines are from *rime-intro.txt*:

```
THE RIME OF THE ANCYENT MARINERE, IN SEVEN PARTS.

ARGUMENT.

How a Ship having passed the Line was driven by Storms to the cold
Country towards the South Pole; and how from thence she made her course
to the tropical Latitude of the Great Pacific Ocean; and of the strange
things that befell; and in what manner the Ancyent Marinere came back to
his own Country.
```

I.

```
1      It is an ancyent Marinere,
2         And he stoppeth one of three:
3      "By thy long grey beard and thy glittering eye
4         "Now wherefore stoppest me?
```

Copy and paste the lines shown here into the lower text box in RegExr. You'll find the file *rime-intro.txt* at Github at *https://github.com/michaeljamesfitzgerald/Introducing-Regular-Expressions*. You'll also find the same file in the download archive found at *http://examples.oreilly.com/9781449392680/examples.zip*. You can also find the text online at Project Gutenberg, but without the numbered lines (see *http://www.gutenberg.org/ebooks/9622*).

Matching String Literals

The most outright, obvious feature of regular expressions is matching strings with one or more literal characters, called *string literals* or just *literals*.

The way to match literal strings is with normal, literal characters. Sounds familiar, doesn't it? This is similar to the way you might do a search in a word processing program or when submitting a keyword to a search engine. When you search for a string of text, character for character, you are searching with a string literal.

If you want to match the word *Ship*, for example, which is a word (string of characters) you'll find early in the poem, just type the word *Ship* in the box at the top of Regexpal, and then the word will be highlighted in the lower text box. (Be sure to capitalize the word.)

Did light blue highlighting show up below? You should be able to see the highlighting in the lower box. If you can't see it, check what you typed again.

 By default, string matching is case-sensitive in Regexpal. If you want to match both lower- and uppercase, click the checkbox next to the words *Case insensitive* at the top left of Regexpal. If you click this box, both *Ship* and *ship* would match if either was present in the target text.

Matching Digits

In the top-left text box in RegExr, enter this character shorthand to match the digits:

\d

This matches all the Arabic digits in the text area below because the *global* checkbox is selected. Uncheck that checkbox, and \d will match only the first occurrence of a digit. (See Figure 2-2.)

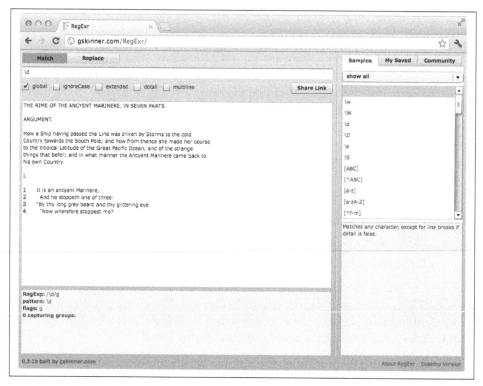

Figure 2-2. Matching all digits in RegExr with \d

Now in place of \d use a character class that matches the same thing. Enter the following range of digits in the top text box of RegExr:

    [0-9]

As you can see in Figure 2-3, though the syntax is different, using \d does the same thing as \[0-9\].

You'll learn more about character classes in Chapter 5.

The character class \[0-9\] is a *range*, meaning that it will match the range of digits 0 through 9. You could also match digits 0 through 9 by listing all the digits:

    [0123456789]

If you want to match only the binary digits 0 and 1, you would use this character class:

```
[01]
```

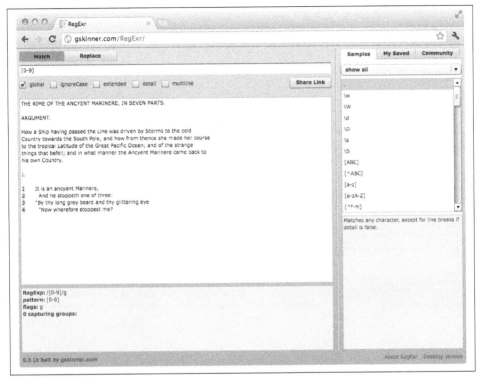

Figure 2-3. Matching all digits in RegExr with [0-9]

Try \[12\] in RegExr and look at the result. With a character class, you can pick the exact digits you want to match. The character shorthand for digits (\d) is shorter and simpler, but it doesn't have the power or flexibility of the character class. I use character classes when I can't use \d (it's not always supported) and when I need to get very specific about what digits I need to match; otherwise, I use \d because it's a simpler, more convenient syntax.

Matching Non-Digits

As is often the case with shorthands, you can flip-flop—that is, you can go the other way. For example, if you want to match characters that are not digits, use this shorthand with an uppercase *D*:

```
\D
```

Try this shorthand in RegExr now. An uppercase *D*, rather than a lowercase, matches non-digit characters (check Figure 2-4). This shorthand is the same as the following character class, a negated class (a negated class says in essence, "don't match these" or "match all but these"):

```
[^0-9]
```

which is the same as:

```
[^\d]
```

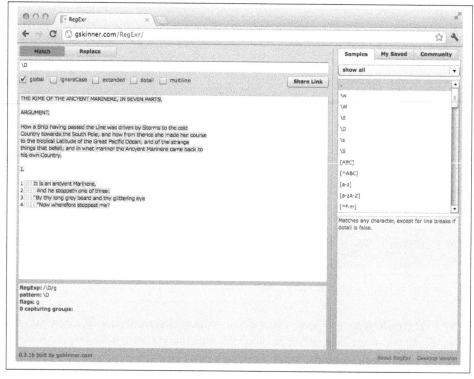

Figure 2-4. Matching non-digits in RegExr with \D

Matching Word and Non-Word Characters

In RegExr, now swap \D with:

```
\w
```

This shorthand will match all word characters (if the *global* option is still checked). The difference between \D and \w is that \D matches whitespace, punctuation, quotation marks, hyphens, forward slashes, square brackets, and other similar characters, while \w does not—it matches letters and numbers.

In English, \w matches essentially the same thing as the character class:

```
[_a-zA-Z0-9]
```

 This character class is limited to a range of characters in the ASCII character set, excluding control characters. You'll learn how to match characters beyond the ASCII set in Chapter 6.

Now to match a non-word character, use an uppercase *W*:

```
\W
```

This shorthand matches whitespace, punctuation, and other kinds of characters that aren't used in words in this example. It is the same as using the following character class:

```
[^_a-zA-Z0-9]
```

Character classes, granted, allow you more control over what you match, but sometimes you don't want or need to type out all those characters. This is known as the "fewest keystrokes win" principle. But sometimes you must type all that stuff out to get precisely what you want. It is your choice.

Just for fun, in RegExr try both:

```
[^\w]
```

and:

```
[^\W]
```

Do you see the differences in what they match?

Table 2-1 provides an extended list of character shorthands. Not all of these work in every regex processor.

Table 2-1. Character shorthands

Character Shorthand	Description
\a	Alert
\b	Word boundary
[\b]	Backspace character
\B	Non-word boundary
\c *x*	Control character
\d	Digit character
\D	Non-digit character
\d *xxx*	Decimal value for a character
\f	Form feed character

Character Shorthand	Description
\r	Carriage return
\n	Newline character
\o *xxx*	Octal value for a character
\s	Space character
\S	Non-space character
\t	Horizontal tab character
\v	Vertical tab character
\w	Word character
\W	Non-word character
\0	Nul character
\ *xxx*	Hexadecimal value for a character
\u *xxxx*	Unicode value for a character

Matching Whitespace

To match whitespace, you can use this shorthand:

    \s

Try this in RegExr and see what lights up (see Figure 2-5). The following character class matches the same thing as \s:

    [\t\n\r]

In other words, it matches:

- Spaces
- Tabs (\t)
- Line feeds (\n)
- Carriage returns (\r)

 Spaces and tabs are highlighted in RegExr, but not line feeds or carriage returns.

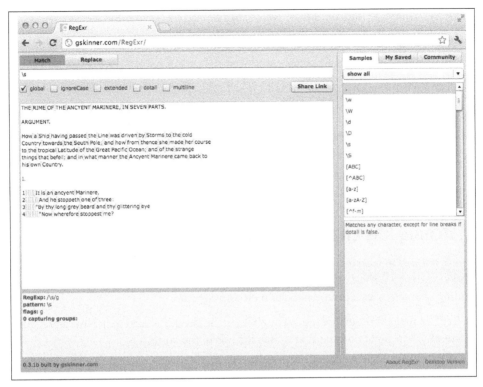

Figure 2-5. Matching whitespace in RegExr with \s

As you can imagine, \s has its *compañero*. To match a non-whitespace character, use:

    \S

This matches everything except whitespace. It matches the character class:

    [^ \t\n\r]

Or:

    [^\s]

Test these out in RegExr to see what happens.

In addition to those characters matched by \s, there are other, less common whitespace characters. Table 2-2 lists character shorthands for common whitespace characters and a few that are more rare.

Table 2-2. Character shorthands for whitespace characters

Character Shorthand	Description
\f	Form feed
\h	Horizontal whitespace
\H	Not horizontal whitespace
\n	Newline
\r	Carriage return
\t	Horizontal tab
\v	Vertical tab (whitespace)
\V	Not vertical whitespace

Matching Any Character, Once Again

There is a way to match *any* character with regular expressions and that is with the dot, also known as a period or a full stop (U+002E). The dot matches all characters but line ending characters, except under certain circumstances.

In RegExr, turn off the *global* setting by clicking the checkbox next to it. Now any regular expression will match on the first match it finds in the target.

Now to match a single character, any character, just enter a single dot in the top text box of RegExr.

In Figure 2-6, you see that the dot matches the first character in the target, namely, the letter *T*.

If you wanted to match the entire phrase *THE RIME*, you could use eight dots:

        . . . .

But this isn't very practical, so I don't recommend using a series of dots like this often, if ever. Instead of eight dots, use a quantifier:

    .{8}

and it would match the first two words and the space in between, but crudely so. To see what I mean by *crudely*, click the checkbox next to *global* and see how useless this really is. It matches sequences of eight characters, end on end, all but the last few characters of the target.

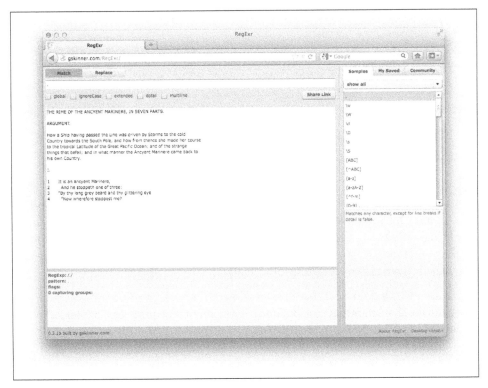

Figure 2-6. Matching a single character in RegExr with "."

Let's try a different tack with word boundaries and starting and ending letters. Type the following in the upper text box of RegExr to see a slight difference:

```
\bA.{5}T\b
```

This expression has a bit more specificity. (Try saying *specificity* three times, out loud.) It matches the word *ANCYENT*, an archaic spelling of *ancient*. How?

- The shorthand \b matches a word boundary, without consuming any characters.
- The characters *A* and *T* also bound the sequence of characters.
- .{5} matches any five characters.
- Match another word boundary with \b.

This regular expression would actually match both *ANCYENT* or *ANCIENT*.

Now try it with a shorthand:

```
\b\w{7}\b
```

Finally, I'll talk about matching zero or more characters:

```
.*
```

which is the same as:

```
[^\n]
```

or:

```
[^\n\r]
```

Similar to this is the dot used with the one or more quantifier (+):

```
.+
```

Try these in RegExr and they will, either of them, match the first line (uncheck *global*). The reason why is that, normally, the dot does not match newline characters, such as a line feed (U+000A) or a carriage return (U+000D). Click the checkbox next to *dotall* in RegExr, and then .* or .+ will match *all* the text in the lower box. (*dotall* means a dot will match all characters, including newlines.)

The reason why it does this is because these quantifiers are *greedy*; in other words, they match all the characters they can. But don't worry about that quite yet. Chapter 7 explains quantifiers and greediness in more detail.

Marking Up the Text

"The Rime of the Ancient Mariner" is just plain text. What if you wanted to display it on the Web? What if you wanted to mark it up as HTML5 using regular expressions, rather than by hand? How would you do that?

In some of the following chapters, I'll show you ways to do this. I'll start out small in this chapter and then add more and more markup as you go along.

In RegExr, click the Replace tab, check *multiline*, and then, in the first text box, enter:

```
(^T.*$)
```

Beginning at the top of the file, this will match the first line of the poem and then capture that text in a group using parentheses. In the next box, enter:

```
<h1>$1</h1>
```

The replacement regex surrounds the captured group, represented by $1, in an *h1* element. You can see the result in the lowest text area. The $1 is a backreference, in Perl style. In most implementations, including Perl, you use this style: \1; but RegExr supports only $1, $2, $3 and so forth. You'll learn more about groups and backreferences in Chapter 4.

Using *sed* to Mark Up Text

On a command line, you could also do this with *sed*. *sed* is a Unix streaming editor that accepts regular expressions and allows you to transform text. It was first developed in the early 1970s by Lee McMahon at Bell Labs. If you are on the Mac or have a Linux box, you already have it.

Test out *sed* at a shell prompt (such as in a Terminal window on a Mac) with this line:

```
echo Hello | sed s/Hello/Goodbye/
```

This is what should have happened:

- The *echo* command prints the word *Hello* to standard output (which is usually just your screen), but the vertical bar (|) pipes it to the *sed* command that follows.
- This pipe directs the output of *echo* to the input of *sed*.
- The *s* (substitute) command of *sed* then changes the word *Hello* to *Goodbye*, and *Goodbye* is displayed on your screen.

If you don't have *sed* on your platform already, at the end of this chapter you'll find some technical notes with some pointers to installation information. You'll find discussed there two versions of *sed*: BSD and GNU.

Now try this: At a command or shell prompt, enter:

```
sed -n 's/^/<h1>/;s/$/<\/h1>/p;q' rime.txt
```

And the output will be:

```
<h1>THE RIME OF THE ANCYENT MARINERE, IN SEVEN PARTS.</h1>
```

Here is what the regex did, broken down into parts:

- The line starts by invoking the *sed* program.
- The -n option suppresses *sed*'s default behavior of echoing each line of input to the output. This is because you want to see only the line effected by the regex, that is, line 1.
- s/^/<h1>/ places an *h1* start-tag at the beginning (\^) of the line.
- The semicolon (;) separates commands.
- s/$/<\/h1>/ places an *h1* end-tag at the end ($) of the line.
- The *p* command prints the affected line (line 1). This is in contrast to -n, which echoes every line, regardless.
- Lastly, the *q* command quits the program so that *sed* processes only the first line.
- All these operations are performed against the file *rime.txt*.

Another way of writing this line is with the -e option. The -e option appends the editing commands, one after another. I prefer the method with semicolons, of course, because it's shorter:

```
sed -ne 's/^/<h1>/' -e 's/$/<\/h1>/p' -e 'q' rime.txt
```

You could also collect these commands in a file, as with *h1.sed* shown here (this file is in the code repository mentioned earlier):

```
#!/usr/bin/sed

s/^/<h1>/
s/$/<\/h1>/
q
```

To run it, type:

```
sed -f h1.sed rime.txt
```

at a prompt in the same directory or folder as *rime.txt*.

Using Perl to Mark Up Text

Finally, I'll show you how to do a similar process with Perl. Perl is a general purpose programming language created by Larry Wall back in 1987. It's known for its strong support of regular expressions and its text processing capabilities.

Find out if Perl is already on your system by typing this at a command prompt, followed by Return or Enter:

```
perl -v
```

This should return the version of Perl on your system or an error (see "Technical Notes" (page 28)).

To accomplish the same output as shown in the *sed* example, enter this line at a prompt:

```
perl -ne 'if ($. == 1) { s/^/<h1>/; s/$/<\/h1>/m; print; }' rime.txt
```

and, as with the *sed* example, you will get this result:

```
<h1>THE RIME OF THE ANCYENT MARINERE, IN SEVEN PARTS.</h1>
```

Here is what happened in the Perl command, broken down again into pieces:

- *perl* invokes the Perl program.
- The -n option loops through the input (the file *rime.txt*).
- The -e option allows you to submit program code on the command line, rather than from a file (like *sed*).
- The *if* statement checks to see if you are on line 1. $. is a special variable in Perl that matches the current line.

- The first substitute command *s* finds the beginning of the first line (\^) and inserts an *h1* start-tag there.

- The second substitute command searches for the end of the line ($), and then inserts an *h1* end-tag.

- The *m* or *multiline* modifier or flag at the end of the substitute command indicates that you are treating this line distinctly and separately; consequently, the $ matches the end of line 1, not the end of the file.

- At last, it prints the result to standard output (the screen).

- All these operations are performed again the file *rime.txt*.

You could also hold all these commands in a program file, such as this file, *h1.pl*, found in the example archive:

```
#!/usr/bin/perl -n

if ($. == 1) {
   s/^/<h1&>;
   s/$/<\/h1>/m;
   print;
}
```

And then, in the same directory as *rime.txt*, run the program like this:

```
perl h1.pl rime.txt
```

There are a lot of ways you can do things in Perl. I am not saying this is the most efficient way to add these tags. It is simply one way. Chances are, by the time this book is in print, I'll think of other, more efficient ways to do things with Perl (and other tools). I hope you will, too.

In the next chapter, we'll talk about boundaries and what are known as *zero-width assertions*.

What You Learned in Chapter 2

- How to match string literals
- How to match digits and non-digits
- What the *global* mode is
- How character shorthands compare with character classes
- How to match word and non-word characters
- How to match whitespace

- How to match any character with the dot
- What the *dotall* mode is
- How to insert HTML markup to a line of text using RegExr, *sed*, and Perl

Technical Notes

- RegExr is found at *http://www.gskinner.com/RegExr* and also has a desktop version (*http://www.gskinner.com/RegExr/desktop/*). RegExr was built in Flex 3 (*http://www.adobe.com/products/flex.html*) and relies on the ActionScript regular expression engine (*http://www.adobe.com/devnet/actionscript.html*). Its regular expressions are similar to those used by JavaScript (see *https://developer.mozilla.org/en/JavaScript/Reference/Global_Objects/RegExp*).

- Git is a fast version control system (*http://git-scm.com*). GitHub is a web-based repository for projects using Git (*http://github.com*). I suggest using the GitHub repository for samples in this book only if you feel comfortable with Git or with other modern version control systems, like Subversion or Mercurial.

- HTML5 (*http://www.w3.org/TR/html5/*) is the fifth major revision of the W3C's HTML, the markup language for publishing on the World Wide Web. It has been in draft for several years and changes regularly, but it is widely accepted as the heir apparent of HTML 4.01 and XHTML.

- *sed* is readily available on Unix/Linux systems, including the Mac (Darwin or BSD version). It is also available on Windows through distributions like Cygwin (*http://www.cygwin.com*) or individually at *http://gnuwin32.sourceforge.net/packages/sed.htm* (currently at version 4.2.1, see *http://www.gnu.org/software/sed/manual/sed.html*).

- To use the Perl examples in this chapter, you may have to install Perl on your system. It comes by default with Mac OS X Lion and often is on Linux systems. If you are on Windows, you can get Perl by installing the appropriate Cygwin packages (see *http://www.cygwin.com*) or by downloading the latest package from the ActiveState website (go to *http://www.activestate.com/activeperl/downloads*). For detailed information on installing Perl, visit *http://learn.perl.org/installing/* or *http://www.perl.org/get.html*.

To find out if you already have Perl, enter the command below at a shell prompt. To do this, open a command or shell window on your system, such as a Terminal window (under Applications/Utilities) on the Mac or a Windows command line window (open Start, and then enter *cmd* in the text box at the bottom of the menu). At the prompt, type:

```
perl -v
```

If Perl is alive and well on your system, then this command will return version information for Perl. On my Mac running Lion, I've installed the latest version of Perl (5.16.0 at the time of this writing) from source and compiled it (see *http://www.cpan.org/src/5.0/perl-5.16.0.tar.gz*). I get the following information back when I enter the command above:

```
This is perl 5, version 16, subversion 0 (v5.16.0) built for darwin-2level

Copyright 1987-2012, Larry Wall

Perl may be copied only under the terms of either the Artistic License or the
GNU General Public License, which may be found in the Perl 5 source kit.

Complete documentation for Perl, including FAQ lists, should be found on
this system using "man perl" or "perldoc perl".  If you have access to the
Internet, point your browser at http://www.perl.org/, the Perl Home Page.
```

Both `perl` and `perldoc` are installed at /usr/local/bin when compiled and built from source, which you can add to your path. For information on setting your path variable, see *http://java.com/en/download/help/path.xml*.

CHAPTER 3

Boundaries

This chapter focuses on assertions. Assertions mark boundaries, but they don't consume characters—that is, characters will not be returned in a result. They are also known as *zero-width assertions*. A zero-width assertion doesn't match a character, per se, but rather a location in a string. Some of these, such as \^ and $, are also called *anchors*.

The boundaries I'll talk about in this chapter are:

- The beginning and end of a line or string
- Word boundaries (two kinds)
- The beginning and end of a subject
- Boundaries that quote string literals

To start, I'll use RegExr again, but this time, for variety, I'll use the Safari browser (however, you can use any browser you like). I'll also use the same text I used last time: the first 12 lines of *rime.txt*. Open the Safari browser with *http://gskinner.com/regexr* and copy the first 12 lines of *rime.txt* from the code archive into the lower box (see Figure 3-1).

The Beginning and End of a Line

As you have seen a number of times already, to match the beginning of a line or string, use the caret or circumflex (U+005E):

```
^
```

Depending on the context, a \^ will match the beginning of a line or string, sometimes a whole document. The context depends on your application and what options you are using with that application.

To match the end of a line or string, as you know, use the dollar sign:

```
$
```

In RegExr, make sure that *multiline* and *dotall* are checked. *global* is checked by default when you open RegExr, but you can leave it checked or unchecked for this example. When *multiline* is not checked, the entire target is considered one string, and if *dotall* is not checked, the dot (.) will not match end-of-line characters.

In the upper text box, enter this regular expression:

```
^How.*Country\.$
```

This will match the entire line beginning with the word *How*. Notice that the period or dot at the end is preceded by a backslash. This escapes the dot so that it is interpreted as a literal. If it was not escaped, what would it match? Any character. If you want to match a literal dot, you have to either escape it or put it in a character class (see Chapter 5).

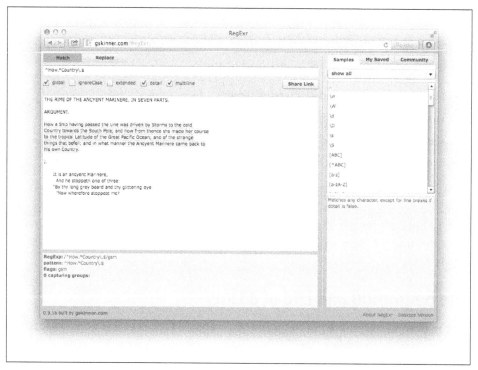

Figure 3-1. RegExr in Safari

If you uncheck *multiline*, then what happens? The highlighting is turned off. With it unchecked and *dotall* checked, enter:

```
^THE.*\?$
```

and you'll see that it matches all the text.

The *dotall* option means that the dot will match newlines in addition to all other characters. Uncheck *dotall*, and the expression matches nothing. However, the following:

```
^THE.*
```

will match the first line. Click *dotall* again, and all text is matched again. The \?$ is not required to match to the end of the text.

Word and Non-word Boundaries

You have already seen \b used several times. It marks a word boundary. Try:

```
\bTHE\b
```

and it will match both occurrences of *THE* in the first line (with *global* checked). Like, \^ or $, \b is a zero-width assertion. It may appear to match things like a space or the beginning of a line, but in actuality, what it matches is a zero-width nothing. Did you notice that the spaces around the second *THE* are not highlighted? That is because they are not part of the match. Not the easiest thing to grasp, but you'll get it by seeing what it does and does not do.

You can also match non-word boundaries. A non-word boundary matches locations that are not equivalent to a word boundary, like a letter or a number within a word or string. To match a non-word boundary, give this a spin:

```
\Be\B
```

and watch what it matches (see Figure 3-2). You'll see that it matches a lowercase *e* when it is surrounded by other letters or non-word characters. Being a zero-width assertion, it does not match the surrounding characters, but it recognizes when the literal *e* is surrounded by non-word boundaries.

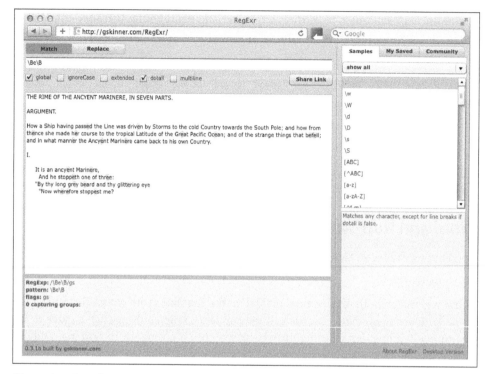

Figure 3-2. Matching non-word boundaries with \B

In some applications, another way for specifying a word boundary is with:

    \<

for the beginning of a word, and with:

    \>

for the end of the word. This is an older syntax, not available in most recent regex applications. It is useful in some instances because, unlike \b, which matches *any* word boundary, this syntax allows you to match either the beginning or ending of a word.

If you have *vi* or *vim* on your system, you can try this out with that editor. Just follow these steps. They're easy even if you have never used *vim* before. In a command or shell window, change directories to where the poem is located and then open it with:

    vim rime.txt

Then enter the following search command:

    /\>

and press Enter or Return. The forward slash (/) is the way you begin a search in *vim*. Watch the cursor and you'll see that this search will find the ends of words. Press *n* to repeat the search. Next enter:

```
/\<
```

followed by Enter or Return. This time the search will find the beginning of words. To exit *vim*, just type ZZ.

This syntax also works with *grep*. Since the early 1970s, *grep* like *sed* has been a Unix mainstay. (In the 1980s, I had a coworker who had a vanity license plate that said *GREP*.) You can learn more about *grep* by typing either:

```
man grep
```

or:

```
info grep
```

at a shell prompt. To get started, try this command at a prompt:

```
grep -Eoc '\<(THE|The|the)\>' rime.txt
```

The *-E* option indicates that you want to use extended regular expressions (EREs) rather than the basic regular expressions (BREs) which are used by *grep* by default. The -o option means you want to show in the result only that part of the line that matches the pattern, and the -c option means only return a count of the result. The pattern in single quotes will match either *THE*, *The*, or *the* as whole words. That's what the < and > help you find.

This command will return:

```
259
```

which is the count of the words found.

On the other hand, if you don't include the < and >, you get a different result. Do it this way:

```
grep -Eoc '(THE|The|the)' rime.txt
```

and you will get a different number:

```
327
```

Why? Because the pattern will match only whole words, plus *any* sequence of characters that contain the word. So that is one reason why the < and > can come in handy.

Other Anchors

Similar to the \^ anchor is the following, a shorthand that matches the start of a subject:

```
\A
```

This is not available with all regex implementations, but you can get it with Perl and PCRE (Perl Compatible Regular Expressions), for example. To match the end of a subject, you can use \A's companion:

```
\Z
```

Also, in some contexts:

```
\z
```

pcregrep is a version of *grep* for the PCRE library. (See "Technical Notes" (page 41) to find out where to get it.) Once installed, to try this syntax with *pcregrep*, you could do something like this:

```
pcregrep -c '\A\s*(THE|The|the)' rime.txt
```

which will return a count (-c) of 108 occurrences of the word *the* (in three cases) which occur near the beginning of a line, preceded by whitespace (zero or more). Next enter this command:

```
pcregrep -n '(MARINERE|Marinere)(.)?\Z' rime.txt
```

This matches either *MARINERE* or *Marinere* at the end of a line (subject) and is followed by any optional character, which in this case is either a punctuation mark or the letter *S*. (The parentheses around the dot are not essential.)

You'll see this output:

```
9:      It is an ancyent Marinere,
37:        The bright-eyed Marinere.
63:        The bright-eyed Marinere.
105:    "God save thee, ancyent Marinere!
282:    "I fear thee, ancyent Marinere!
702:    He loves to talk with Marineres
```

The -n option with *pcregrep* gives you the line numbers at the beginning of each line of output. The command line options of *pcregrep* are very similar to those of *grep*. To see them, do:

```
pcregrep --help
```

Quoting a Group of Characters as Literals

You can use these sequences to quote a set of characters as literals:

```
\Q
```

and:

```
\E
```

To show you how this works, enter the following metacharacters in the lower box of RegExr:

.^$*+?|(){}[]\-

These 15 metacharacters are treated as special characters in regular expressions, used for encoding a pattern. (The hyphen is treated specially, as signifying a range, inside of the square brackets of a character class. Otherwise, it's not special.)

If you try to match those characters in the upper text box of RegExr, nothing will happen. Why? Because RegExr thinks (if it can think) that you are entering a regular expression, not literal characters. Now try:

\Q$\E

and it will match $ because anything between \Q and \E is interpreted as a literal character (see Figure 3-3). (Remember, you can precede a metacharacer with a \ to make it literal.)

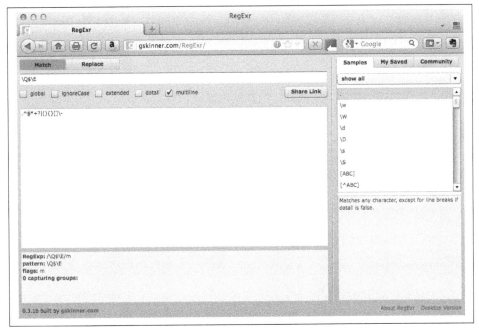

Figure 3-3. Quoting metacharacters as literals

Adding Tags

In RegExr, uncheck *global* and check *multiline*, click the Replace tab, and then, in the first text box (marked number 1 in Figure 3-4), enter:

```
^(.*)$
```

This will match and capture the first line of text. Then in the next box (marked number 2), enter this or something similar:

```
<!DOCTYPE html>\n<html lang="en">\n<head><title>Rime</title></head>\n<body>\n
    <h1>$1</h1>
```

As you enter the replacement text, you'll notice that the subject text (shown in the box marked number 3) is changed in the results text box (marked number 4), to include the markup you've added (see Figure 3-4).

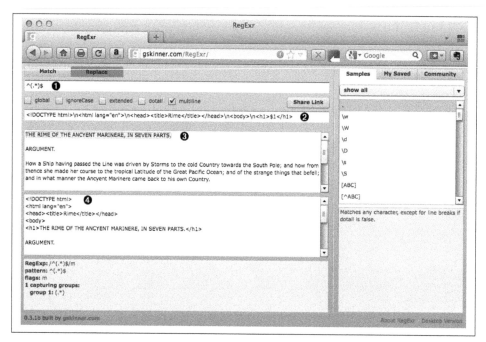

Figure 3-4. Adding markup with RegExr

RegExr does well to demonstrate one way to do this, but it is limited in what it can do. For example, it can't save any results out to a file. We have to look beyond the browser for that.

Adding Tags with *sed*

On a command line, you could also do something similar to what we just did in RegExr with *sed*, which you saw in the last chapter. The insert (i) command in *sed* allows you to insert text above or before a location in a document or a string. By the way, the opposite of *i* in *sed* is *a*, which appends text below or after a location. We'll use the append command later.

The following command inserts the HTML5 doctype and several other tags, beginning at line 1:

```
sed '1 i\
<!DOCTYPE html>\
<html lang=\"en\">\
<head&gt;\
<title>Rime</title>\
</head>\
<body>

s/^/<h1>/
s/$/<\/h1>/
q' rime.txt
```

The backslashes (\) at the end of the lines allow you to insert newlines into the stream and not execute the command prematurely. The backslashes in front of the quotation marks *escape* the quotes so that they are seen as literal characters, not part of the command.

When you run this *sed* command correctly, this is what your output will look like:

```
<!DOCTYPE html>
<html lang="en">
<head>
<title>The Rime of the Ancyent Mariner (1798)</title>
</head>
<body>
<h1>THE RIME OF THE ANCYENT MARINERE, IN SEVEN PARTS.</h1>
```

These same *sed* commands are saved in the file *top.sed* in the example archive. You can run this on the file using this command:

```
sed -f top.sed rime.txt
```

You should get the same output as you saw in the previous command. If you want to save the output to a file, you can redirect the output to a file, like so:

```
sed -f top.sed rime.txt &gt; temp
```

In addition to showing the result on the screen, this redirect part of the command (> temp) will save the output to the file *temp*.

Adding Tags with Perl

Let's try to accomplish this same thing with Perl. Without explaining everything that's going on, just try this:

```
perl -ne 'print "<!DOCTYPE html>\
<html lang=\"en\">\
<head><title>Rime</title></head>\
<body>\
" if $. == 1;
s/^/<h1>/;s/$/<\/h1>/m;print;exit;' rime.txt
```

Compare this with the *sed* command. How is it similar? How is it different? The *sed* command is a little simpler, but Perl is a lot more powerful, in my opinion.

Here is how it works:

- The $. variable, which is tested with the *if* statement, represents the current line. The *if* statement returns *true*, meaning it passes the test that the current line is line 1.

- When Perl finds line 1 with *if*, it prints the doctype and a few HTML tags. It is necessary to escape the quote marks as in *sed*.

- The first substitution inserts an *h1* start-tag at the beginning of the line, and the second one inserts an *h1* end-tag at the end of the line. The *m* at the end of the second substitution means that it uses a *multiline* modifier. This is done so that the command recognizes the end of the first line. Without *m*, the *$* would match to the end of the file.

- The *print* command prints the result of the substitutions.

- The *exit* command exits Perl immediately. Otherwise, because of -n option, it would loop through every line of the file, which we don't want for this script.

That was a lot of typing, so I put all that Perl code in a file and called it *top.pl*, also found in the code archive:

```
#!/usr/bin/perl -n

if ($ == 1) {
print "<!DOCTYPE html>\
<html lang=\"en\">\
<head>\
<title>The Rime of the Ancyent Mariner (1798)</title>\
</head>\
<body>\
";
s/^/<h1>/;
```

```
s/$/<\/h1>/m;
print;
exit;
}
```

Run this with:

```
perl top.pl rime.txt
```

You get a similar output as in the previous command, though it is formed a little differently. (You can redirect the output with >, as with *sed*.)

The next chapter covers alternation, groups, and backreferences, among other things. See you over there.

What You Learned in Chapter 3

- How to use anchors at the beginning or end of a line with \^ or $
- How to use word boundaries and non-word boundaries
- How to match the beginning or end of a subject with \A and \Z (or \z)
- How to quote strings as literals with \Q and \E
- How to add tags to a document with RegExr, *sed*, and Perl

Technical Notes

- *vi* is a Unix editor developed in 1976 by Sun cofounder Bill Joy that uses regular expressions. The *vim* editor is a replacement for *vi*, developed primarily by Bram Moolenaar (see *http://www.vim.org*). An early paper on *vi* by Bill Joy and Mark Horton is found here: *http://docs.freebsd.org/44doc/usd/12.vi/paper.html*. The first time I used *vi* was in 1983, and I use it nearly every day. It lets me to do more things more quickly than with any other text editor. And it is so powerful that I am always discovering new features that I never knew about, even though I've been acquainted with it for nearly 30 years.

- *grep* is a Unix command-line utility for searching and printing strings with regular expressions. Invented by Ken Thompson in 1973, *grep* is said to have grown out of the *ed* editor command g/re/p (global/regular expression/print). It was superseded but not retired by *egrep* (or *grep -E*), which uses extended regular expressions (EREs) and has additional metacharacters such as |, +, ?, (, and). *fgrep* (*grep -F*) searches files using literal strings; metacharacters like $, *, and | don't have special meaning. *grep* is available on Linux systems as well as the Mac OS X's Darwin. You can also get it as part of the Cygwin GNU distribution (*http://www.cygwin.com*) or you can download it from *http://gnuwin32.sourceforge.net/packages/grep.htm*.

- PCRE (*http://www.pcre.org*) or Perl Compatible Regular Expressions is a C library of functions (8-bit and 16-bit) for regular expressions that are compatible with Perl 5, and include some features of other implementations. *pcregrep* is an 8-bit, *grep*-like tool that enables you to use the features of the PCRE library on the command line. You can get *pcregrep* for the Mac through Macports (*http://www.macports.org*) by running the command `sudo port install pcre`. (Xcode is a prerequisite; see *https://developer.apple.com/technologies/tools/*. Login required.)

CHAPTER 4

Alternation, Groups, and Backreferences

You have already seen groups in action. Groups surround text with parentheses to help perform some operation, such as the following:

- Performing alternation, a choice between two or more optional patterns
- Creating subpatterns
- Capturing a group to later reference with a backreference
- Applying an operation to a grouped pattern, such as a quantifer
- Using non-capturing groups
- Atomic grouping (advanced)

We'll be using a few contrived examples, in addition to the text from "The Rime of the Ancyent Mariner" again, in *rime.txt*. This time, I'll use the desktop version of RegExr, as well as other tools like *sed*. You can download the desktop version of RegExr from *http://www.regexr.com*, for Windows, Mac, or Linux (it was written with Adobe AIR). Click the Desktop Version link on the RegExr web page (lower-right corner) for more information.

Alternation

Simply said, *alternation* gives you a choice of alternate patterns to match. For example, let's say you wanted to find out how many occurrences of the article *the* are in the "The Rime of the Ancient Mariner." The problem is, the word occurs as *THE*, *The*, and *the* in the poem. You can use alternation to deal with this peculiarity.

Open the RegExr desktop application by double-clicking on its icon. It looks very much like the online version but has the advantage of being local on your machine, so you won't suffer the network issues that sometimes occur when using web applications. I've copied and pasted the entire poem in RegExr desktop for the next exercise. I'm using it on a Mac running OS X Lion.

In the top text box, enter the pattern:

```
(the|The|THE)
```

and you'll see all occurrences of *the* in the poem highlighted in the lower box (see Figure 4-1). Use the scroll bar to view more of the result.

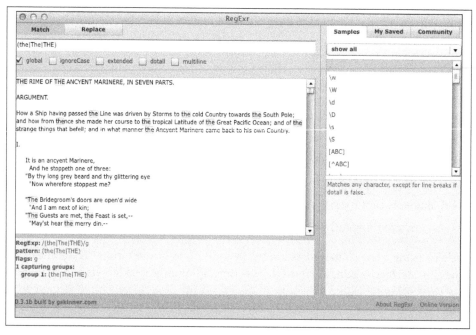

Figure 4-1. Using alternation in RegExr desktop version

We can make this group shorter by applying an option. Options let you specify the way you would like to search for a pattern. For example, the option:

```
(?i)
```

makes your pattern case-insensitive, so instead of using the original pattern with alternation, you can do this instead:

```
(?i)the
```

Try this in RegExr to see how it works. You can also specify case-insensitivity by checking *ignoreCase* in RegExr, but both will work. This and other options or modifiers are listed in Table 4-1.

Table 4-1. Options in regular expressions

Option	Description	Supported by
(?d)	Unix lines	Java
(?i)	Case insensitive	PCRE, Perl, Java
(?J)	Allow duplicate names	PCRE[a]
(?m)	Multiline	PCRE, Perl, Java
(?s)	Single line (dotall)	PCRE, Perl, Java
(?u)	Unicode case	Java
(?U)	Default match lazy	PCRE
(?x)	Ignore whitespace, comments	PCRE, Perl, Java
(?-…)	Unset or turn off options	PCRE

[a] See "Named Subpatterns" in *http://www.pcre.org/pcre.txt*.

Let's now use alternation with *grep*. The options in Table 4-1, by the way, don't work with *grep*, so you are going to use the original alternation pattern. To count the number of lines where the word *the* occurs, regardless of case, one or more times, use:

```
grep -Ec "(the|The|THE)" rime.txt
```

and get this answer:

```
327
```

This result does not tell the whole story. Stay tuned.

Here is an analysis of the *grep* command:

- The *-E* option means that you want to use extended regular expressions (EREs) rather than basic regular expressions (BREs). This, for example, saves you from having to escape the parentheses and the vertical bar, like \(THE\|The\|the\), as you must with BREs.
- The *-c* option returns a count of the matched lines (not matched words).
- The parentheses group the choice or alternation of *the*, *The*, or *THE*.
- The vertical bar separates possible choices, which are evaluated left to right.

To get a count of actual words used, this approach will return each occurrence of the word, one per line:

```
grep -Eo "(the|The|THE)" rime.txt | wc -l
```

This returns:

```
412
```

And here is a bit more analysis:

- The -o option means to show only that part of the line that matches the pattern, though this is not apparent due to the pipe (|) to *wc*.
- The vertical bar, in this context, pipes the output of the *grep* command to the input of the *wc* command. *wc* is a word count command, and -l counts the number of lines of the input.

Why the big difference between 327 and 412? Because *-c* gives you a count of matching lines, but there can be more than one match on each line. If you use *-o* with *wc -l*, then each occurrence of the various forms of the word will appear on a separate line and be counted, giving the higher number.

To perform this same match with Perl, write your command this way:

```
perl -ne 'print if /(the|The|THE)/' rime.txt
```

Or better yet, you can do it with the (?i) option mentioned earlier, but without alternation:

```
perl -ne 'print if /(?i)the/' rime.txt
```

Or even better yet, append the *i* modifier after the last pattern delimiter:

```
perl -ne 'print if /the/i' rime.txt
```

and you will get the same outcome. The simpler the better. For a list of additional modifiers (also called *flags*), see Table 4-2. Also, compare options (similar but with a different syntax) in Table 4-1.

Table 4-2. Perl modifiers (flags)[a]

Modifier	Description
a	Match \d, \s, \w, and POSIX in ASCII range only
c	Keep current position after match fails
d	Use default, native rules of the platform
g	Global matching
i	Case-insensitive matching
l	Use current locale's rules
m	Multiline strings
p	Preserve the matched string
s	Treat strings as a single line
u	Use Unicode rules when matching
x	Ignore whitespace and comments

[a] See *http://perldoc.perl.org/perlre.html#Modifiers*.

Subpatterns

Most often, when you refer to *subpatterns* in regular expressions, you are referring to a group or groups within groups. A subpattern is a pattern within a pattern. Often, a condition in a subpattern is matchable when a preceding pattern is matched, but not always. Subpatterns can be designed in a variety of ways, but we're concerned primarily with those defined within parentheses here.

In one sense, the pattern you saw earlier:

```
(the|The|THE)
```

has three subpatterns: *the* is the first subpattern, *The* is the second, and *THE* the third, but matching the second subpattern, in this instance, is not dependent on matching the first. (The leftmost pattern is matched first.)

Now here is one where the subpattern(s) depend on the previous pattern:

```
(t|T)h(e|eir)
```

In plain language, this will match the literal characters *t* or *T* followed by an *h* followed by either an *e* or the letters *eir*. Accordingly, this pattern will match any of:

- *the*
- *The*
- *their*
- *Their*

In this case, the second subpattern (e|eir) is dependent on the first (tT).

Subpatterns don't require parentheses. Here is an example of subpatterns done with character classes:

```
\b[tT]h[ceinry]*\b
```

This pattern can match, in addition to *the* or *The*, words such as *thee*, *thy* and *thence*. The two word boundaries (\b) mean the pattern will match whole words, not letters embedded in other words.

Here is a complete analysis of this pattern:

- \b matches a beginning word boundary.
- \[tT\] is a character class that matches either an lowercase *t* or an uppercase *T*. We can consider this the first subpattern.
- Then the pattern matches (or attempts to match) a lowercase *h*.
- The second or last subpattern is also expressed as a character class \[ceinry\] followed by a quantifier * for zero or more.
- Finally, another word boundary \b ends the pattern.

 One interesting aspect of the state of regular expressions is that terminology, while usually close in meaning, can also range far. In defining *subpattern* and other terms in this book, I've examined a variety of sources and have tried to bring them together under one roof. But I suspect that there are some who would argue that a character class is not a subpattern. My take is they can function as subpatterns, so I lump them in.

Capturing Groups and Backreferences

When a pattern groups all or part of its content into a pair of parentheses, it captures that content and stores it temporarily in memory. You can reuse that content if you wish by using a backreference, in the form:

```
\1
```

or:

```
$1
```

where \1 or $1 reference the first captured group, \2 or $2 reference the second captured group, and so on. *sed* will only accept the \1 form, but Perl accepts both.

Originally, *sed* supported backreferences in the range \1 through \9, but that limitation does not appear to exist any longer.

You have already seen this in action, but I'll demonstrate it here again. We'll use it to rearrange the wording of a line of the poem, with apologies to Samuel Taylor Coleridge. In the top text box in RegExr, after clicking the Replace tab, enter this pattern:

    (It is) (an ancyent Marinere)

Scroll the subject text (third text area) down until you can see the highlighted line, and then in the second box, enter:

    $2 $1

and you'll see in the lowest box the line rearranged as:

    an ancyent Marinere It is,

(See Figure 4-2.)

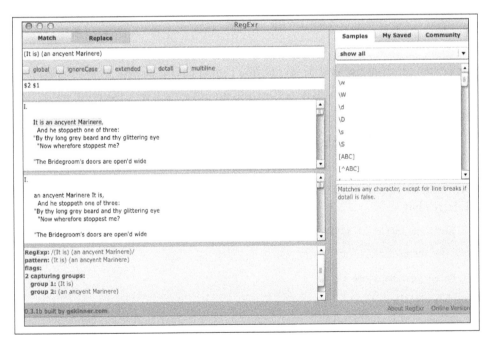

Figure 4-2. Referencing backreferences with $1 and $2

Here is how to accomplish the same result with *sed*:

```
sed -En 's/(It is) (an ancyent Marinere)/\2 \1/p' rime.txt
```

and the output will be:

```
an ancyent Marinere It is,
```

just as in RegExr. Let's analyze the *sed* command to help you understand everything that is going on:

- The *-E* option once again invokes EREs, so you don't have to quote the parentheses, for example.
- The *-n* option suppresses the default behavior of printing every line.
- The substitute command searches for a match for the text "It is an ancyent Marinere," capturing it into two groups.
- The substitute command also replaces the match by rearranging the captured text in the output, with the backreference \2 first, then \1.
- The *p* at the end of the substitute command means you want to print the line.

A similar command in Perl will do the same thing:

```
perl -ne 'print if s/(It is) (an ancyent Marinere)/\2 \1/' rime.txt
```

Notice that this uses the \1 style syntax. You can, of course, use the $1 syntax, too:

```
perl -ne 'print if s/(It is) (an ancyent Marinere)/$2 $1/' rime.txt
```

I like how Perl lets you print a selected line without jumping through hoops.

I'd like to point out something about the output:

```
an ancyent Marinere It is,
```

The capitalization got mixed up in the transformation. Perl can fix that with \u and \l. Here's how:

```
perl -ne 'print if s/(It is) (an ancyent Marinere)/\u$2 \l$1/' rime.txt
```

Now the result looks much better:

```
An ancyent Marinere it is,
```

And here is why:

- The \l syntax does not match anything, but it changes the character that follows to lowercase.
- The \u syntax capitalizes the character that follows it.

- The \U directive (not shown) turns the text string that follows into all uppercase.

- The \L directive (not shown) turns the text string that follows into all lowercase.

These directives remain in effect until another is found (like \l or \E, the end of a quoted string). Experiment with these to see how they work.

Named Groups

Named groups are captured groups with names. You can access those groups by name later, rather than by integer. I'll show you how here in Perl:

```
perl -ne 'print if s/(?<one>It is) (?<two>an ancyent Marinere)/\u$+{two}
    \l$+{one}/' rime.txt
```

Let's look at it:

- Adding ?<one> and ?<two> inside the parentheses names the groups *one* and *two*, respectively.

- $+{one} references the group named *one*, and $+{two}, the group named *two*.

You can also reuse named groups within the pattern where the group was named. I'll show you what I mean. Let's say you were searching for a string that contained six zeros all together:

```
000000
```

It's a shallow example, but serves to show you how this works. So name a group of three zeros with this pattern (the *z* is arbitrary):

```
(?<z>0{3})
```

You can then use the group again like this:

```
(?<z>0{3})\k<z>
```

Or this:

```
(?<z>0{3})\k'z'
```

Or this:

```
(?<z>0{3})\g{z}
```

Try this in RegExr for quick results. All these examples will work. Table 4-3 shows many of the possibilities with named group syntax.

Table 4-3. Named group syntax

Syntax	Description
(?<*name*>...)	A named group
(?*name*...)	Another named group
(?P<*name*>...)	A named group in Python
\k<*name*>	Reference by name in Perl
\k'*name*'	Reference by name in Perl
\g{name}	Reference by name in Perl
\k{name}	Reference by name in .NET
(?P=name)	Reference by name in Python

Non-Capturing Groups

There are also groups that are non-capturing groups—that is, they don't store their content in memory. Sometimes this is an advantage, especially if you never intend to reference the group. Because it doesn't store its content, it is possible it may yield better performance, though performance issues are hardly perceptible when running the simple examples in this book.

Remember the first group discussed in this chapter? Here it is again:

    (the|The|THE)

You don't need to backreference anything, so you could write a non-capturing group this way:

    (?:the|The|THE)

Going back to the beginning of this chapter, you could add an option to make the pattern case-insensitive, like this (though the option obviates the need for a group):

    (?i)(?:the)

Or you could do it this way:

    (?:(?i)the)

Or, better yet, the *pièce de résistance*:

    (?i:the)

The option letter *i* can be inserted between the question mark and the colon.

Atomic Groups

Another kind of non-capturing group is the *atomic group*. If you are using a regex engine that does backtracking, this group will turn backtracking off, not for the entire regular expression but just for that part enclosed in the atomic group. The syntax looks like this:

```
(?>the)
```

When would you want to use atomic groups? One of the things that can really slow regex processing is backtracking. The reason why is, as it tries all the possibilities, it takes time and computing resources. Sometimes it can gobble up a lot of time. When it gets really bad, it's called *catastrophic backtracking*.

You can turn off backtracking altogether by using a non-backtracking engine like re2 (*http://code.google.com/p/re2/*) or by turning it off for parts of your regular expression with atomic grouping.

 My focus in this book is to introduce syntax. I talk very little about performance tuning here. Atomic groups are mainly a performance consideration in my view.

In Chapter 5, you'll learn about character classes.

What You Learned in Chapter 4

- That alternation allows a choice between two or more patterns
- What options modifiers are and how to use them in a pattern
- Different kinds of subpatterns
- How to use capturing groups and backreferences
- How to use named groups and how to reference them
- How to use non-capturing groups.
- A little about atomic grouping.

Technical Notes

- The Adobe AIR runtime lets you use HTML, JavaScript, Flash, and ActionScript to build web applications that run as standalone client applications without having to use a browser. Find out more at *http://www.adobe.com/products/air.html*.

- Python (*http://www.python.org*) is an easy-to-understand, high-level programming language. It has a regular expression implementation (see *http://docs.python.org/library/re.html*).

- .NET (*http://www.microsoft.com/net*) is a programming framework for the Windows platform. It, too, has a regular expression implementation (see *http://msdn.microsoft.com/en-us/library/hs600312.aspx*).

- More advanced explanations of atomic grouping are available at *http://www.regular-expressions.info/atomic.html* and *http://stackoverflow.com/questions/6488944/atomic-group-and-non-capturing-group*.

CHAPTER 5

Character Classes

I'll now talk more about character classes or what are sometimes called *bracketed expressions*. Character classes help you match specific characters, or sequences of specific characters. They can be just as broad or far-reaching as character shorthands—for example, the character shorthand \d will match the same characters as:

```
0-9
```

But you can use character classes to be even more specific than that. In this way, they are more versatile than shorthands.

Try these examples in whatever regex processor you prefer. I'll use Rubular in Opera and Reggy on the desktop.

To do this testing, enter this string in the subject or target area of the web page:

```
! " # $ % & ' ( ) * + , - . /
0     1     2     3     4     5     6     7     8     9
: ; < = > ? @
A B C D E F G H I J K L M N O P Q R S T U V W X Y Z
[ \ ] ^ _ `
a b c d e f g h i j k l m n o p q r s t u v w x y z
{ | } ~
```

You don't have to type all that in. You'll find this text stored in the file *ascii-graphic.txt* in the code archive that comes with this book.

To start out, use a character class to match a set of English characters—in this case, the English vowels:

```
[aeiou]
```

The lowercase vowels should be highlighted in the lower text area (see Figure 5-1). How would you highlight the uppercase vowels? How would you highlight or match both?

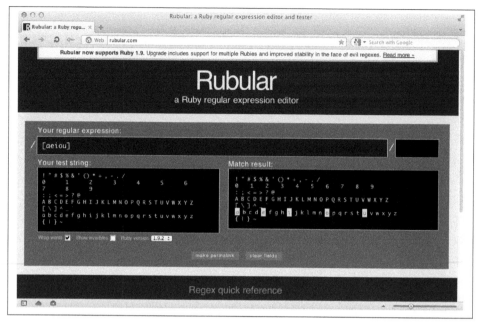

Figure 5-1. Character class with Rubular in the Opera browser

With character classes, you can also match a range of characters:

```
[a-z]
```

This matches the lowercase letters *a* through *z*. Try matching a smaller range of those characters, something like *a* through *f*:

```
[a-f]
```

Of course, you can also specify a range of digits:

```
[0-9]
```

Or an even smaller range such as 3, 4, 5, and 6:

```
[3-6]
```

Now expand your horizon. If you wanted to match even numbers in the range 10 through 19, you could combine two character classes side by side, like this:

```
\b[1][24680]\b
```

Or you could push things further and look for even numbers in the range 0 through 99 with this (yes, as we learned in high school, zero by itself is even):

```
\b[24680]\b|\b[1-9][24680]\b
```

If you want to create a character class that matches hexadecimal digits, how would you do it? Here is a hint:

```
[a-fA-F0-9]
```

You can also use shorthands inside of a character class. For example, to match whitespace and word characters, you could create a character class like this:

```
[\w\s]
```

Which is the same as:

```
[_a-zA-Z \t\n\r]
```

but easier to type.

Negated Character Classes

You have already seen syntax a number of times, so I'll be brief. A negated character class matches characters that do not match the content of the class. For example, if you didn't want to match vowels, you could write (try it in your browser, then see Figure 5-2):

```
[^aeiou]
```

In essence, the caret (\^) at the beginning of the class means "No, I don't want these characters." (The caret *must* appear at the beginning.)

Figure 5-2. Negated character class with RegExr in Opera

Union and Difference

Character classes can act like sets. In fact, one other name for a character class is a *character set*. This functionality is not supported by all implementations. But Java supports it.

I'll now show you a Mac desktop application called Reggy (see "Technical Notes" (page 62)). Under Preferences (Figure 5-3), I changed the Regular Expression Syntax to *Java*, and in Font (under Format), I changed the point size to 24 points for readability.

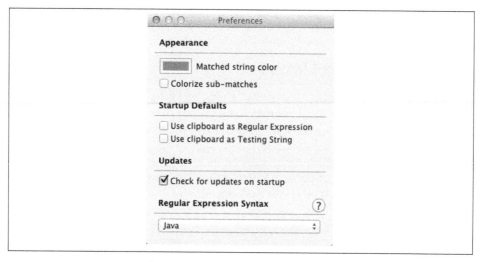

Figure 5-3. Reggy preferences

If you wanted a union of two character sets, you could do it like this:

    [0-3[6-9]]

The regex would match 0 through 3 or 6 through 9. Figure 5-4 shows you how this looks in Reggy.

To match a difference (in essence, subtraction):

    [a-z&&[^m-r]]

which matches all the letters from *a* to *z*, except *m* through *r* (see Figure 5-5).

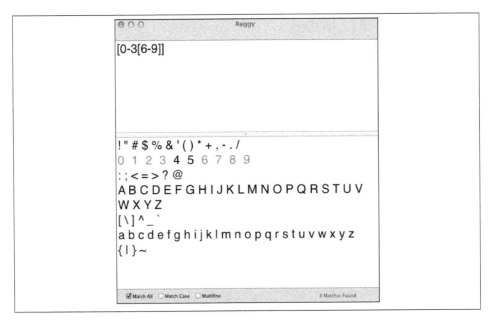

Figure 5-4. Union of two character sets in Reggy

Figure 5-5. Difference of two characters sets in Reggy

POSIX Character Classes

POSIX or Portable Operating System Interface is a family of standards maintained by IEEE. It includes a regular expression standard, (ISO/IEC/IEEE 9945:2009), which provides a set of named character classes that have the form:

    [[:xxxx:]]

where *xxxx* is a name, such as *digit* or *word*.

To match alphanumeric characters (letters and digits), try:

    [[:alnum:]]

Figure 5-6 shows the alphanumeric class in Rubular.

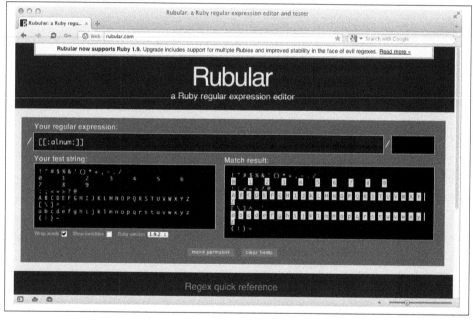

Figure 5-6. POSIX alphanumeric character class in Reggy

An alternative for this is simply the shorthand \w. Which is easier to type, the POSIX character class or the shorthand? You know where I'm going: The least amount of typing wins. I admit I don't use POSIX classes very often. But they're still worth knowing about.

For alphabetic characters in either upper- or lowercase, use:

    [[:alpha:]]

If you want to match characters in the ASCII range, choose:

    [[:ascii:]]

Of course, there are negated POSIX character classes as well, in the form:

    [[:^xxxx:]]

So if you wanted to match non-alphabetic characters, you could use:

    [[:^alpha:]]

To match space and tab characters, do:

    [[:space:]]

Or to match all whitespace characters, there's:

    [[:blank:]]

There are a number of these POSIX character classes, which are shown in Table 5-1.

Table 5-1. POSIX character classes

Character Class	Description
[[:alnum:]]	Alphanumeric characters (letters and digits)
[[:alpha:]]	Alphabetic characters (letters)
[[:ascii:]]	ASCII characters (all 128)
[[:blank:]]	Blank characters
[[:ctrl:]]	Control characters
[[:digit:]]	Digits
[[:graph:]]	Graphic characters
[[:lower:]]	Lowercase letters
[[:print:]]	Printable characters
[[:punct:]]	Punctuation characters
[[:space:]]	Whitespace characters
[[:upper:]]	Uppercase letters
[[:word:]]	Word characters
[[:xdigit:]]	Hexadecimal digits

The next chapter is dedicated to matching Unicode and other characters.

What You Learned in Chapter 5

- How to create a character class or set with a bracketed expression
- How to create one or more ranges within a character class
- How to match even numbers in the range 0 through 99
- How to match a hexadecimal number
- How to use character shorthands within a character class

- How to negate a character class
- How to perform union, and difference with character classes
- What POSIX character classes are

Technical Notes

- The Mac desktop application Reggy can be downloaded for free at *http://www.reggyapp.com*. Reggy shows you what it has matched by changing the color of the matched text. The default is blue, but you can change this color in Preferences under the Reggy menu. Under Preferences, choose Java under Regular Expression Syntax.

- The Opera Next browser, currently in beta, can be downloaded from *http://www.opera.com/browser/next/*.

- Rubular is an online Ruby regular expression editor created by Michael Lovitt that supports both versions 1.8.7 and 1.9.2 of Ruby (see *http://www.rubular.com*).

- Read more about even numbers, of which zero is one, at *http://mathworld.wolfram.com/EvenNumber.html*.

- The Java (1.6) implementation of regular expressions is documented at *http://docs.oracle.com/javase/6/docs/api/java/util/regex/Pattern.html*.

- You can find out more about IEEE and its family of POSIX standards at *http://www.ieee.org*.

CHAPTER 6

Matching Unicode and Other Characters

You will have occasion to match characters or ranges of characters that are outside the scope of ASCII. ASCII, or the American Standard Code for Information Interchange, defines an English character set—the letters A through Z in upper- and lowercase, plus control and other characters. It's been around for a long time: The 128-character Latin-based set was standardized in 1968. That was back before there was such a thing as a personal computer, before VisiCalc, before the mouse, before the Web, but I still look up ASCII charts online regularly.

I remember when I started my career many years ago, I worked with an engineer who kept an ASCII code chart in his wallet. Just in case. The ASCII Code Chart: Don't leave home without it.

So I won't gainsay the importance of ASCII, but now it is dated, especially in light of the Unicode standard (*http://www.unicode.org*), which currently represents over 100,000 characters. Unicode, however, does not leave ASCII in the dust; it incorporates ASCII into its Basic Latin code table (see *http://www.unicode.org/charts/PDF/U0000.pdf*).

In this chapter, you will step out of the province of ASCII into the not-so-new world of Unicode.

The first text is *voltaire.txt* from the code archive, a quote from Voltaire (1694–1778), the French Enlightenment philosopher.

> Qu'est-ce que la tolérance? c'est l'apanage de l'humanité. Nous sommes tous pétris de faiblesses et d'erreurs; pardonnons-nous réciproquement nos sottises, c'est la première loi de la nature.

Here is an English translation:

> What is tolerance? It is the consequence of humanity. We are all formed of frailty and error; let us pardon reciprocally each other's folly—that is the first law of nature.

Matching a Unicode Character

There are a variety of ways you can specify a Unicode character, also known as a code point. (For the purposes of this book, a Unicode character is one that is outside of the range of ASCII, though that is not strictly accurate.)

Start out by placing the Voltaire quote in Regexpal (*http://www.regexpal.com*), and then entering this regular expression:

    \u00e9

The \u is followed by a hexadecimal value 00e9 (this is case insensitive—that is, 00E9 works, too). The value 00e9 is equivalent to the decimal value 233, well out of the ASCII range (0–127).

Notice that the letter *é* (small letter e with an acute accent) is highlighted in Regexpal (see Figure 6-1). That's because *é* is the code point U+00E9 in Unicode, which was matched by \u00e9.

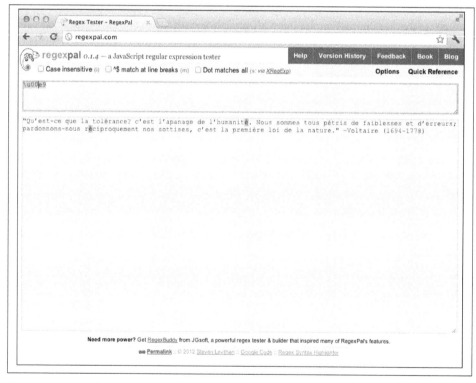

Figure 6-1. Matching U+00E9 in Regexpal

Regexpal uses the JavaScript implementation of regular expressions. JavaScript also allows you to use this syntax:

```
\xe9
```

Try this in Regexpal and see how it matches the same character as `\u00e9`.

Let's try it with a different regex engine. Open *http://regexhero.net/tester/* in a browser. Regex Hero is written in .NET and has a little different syntax. Drop the contents of the file *basho.txt* into the text area labeled Target String. This contains a famous haiku written by the Japanese poet Matsuo Basho (who, coincidentally, died just one week before Voltaire was born).

Here is the poem in Japanese:

```
古池
蛙飛び込む
水の音
        -芭蕉 (1644-1694)
```

And here is a translation in English:

```
At the ancient pond
a frog plunges into
the sound of water.
        —Basho (1644-1694)
```

To match part of the Japanese text, in the text area marked Regular Expression, type the following:

```
\u6c60
```

This is the code point for the Japanese (Chinese) character for *pond*. It will be highlighted below (see Figure 6-2).

While you are here, try matching the em dash (—) with:

```
\u2014
```

Or the en dash (–) with:

```
\u2013
```

Now look at these characters in an editor.

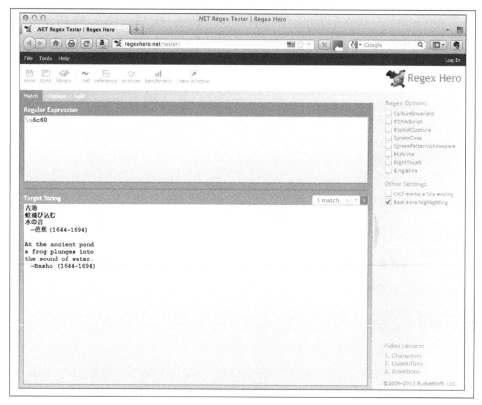

Figure 6-2. Matching U+6c60 in Regex Hero

Using *vim*

If you have *vim* on your system, you can open *basho.txt* with it, as shown:

```
vim basho.txt
```

Now, starting with a slash (\), enter a search with this line:

```
/\%u6c60
```

followed by Enter or Return. The cursor moves to the beginning of the match, as you can see in Figure 6-3. Table 6-1 shows you your options. You can use *x* or *X* following the \% to match values in the range 0–255 (0–FF), *u* to match up to four hexadecimal numbers in the range 256–65,535 (100–FFFF), or *U* to match up to eight characters in the range 65,536–2,147,483,647 (10000–7FFFFFFF). That takes in a lot of code—a lot more than currently exist in Unicode.

Table 6-1. Matching Unicode in Vim

First Character	Maximum Characters	Maximum Value
x or X	2	255 (FF)
u	4	65,535 (FFFF)
U	8	2,147,483,647 (7FFFFFFF)

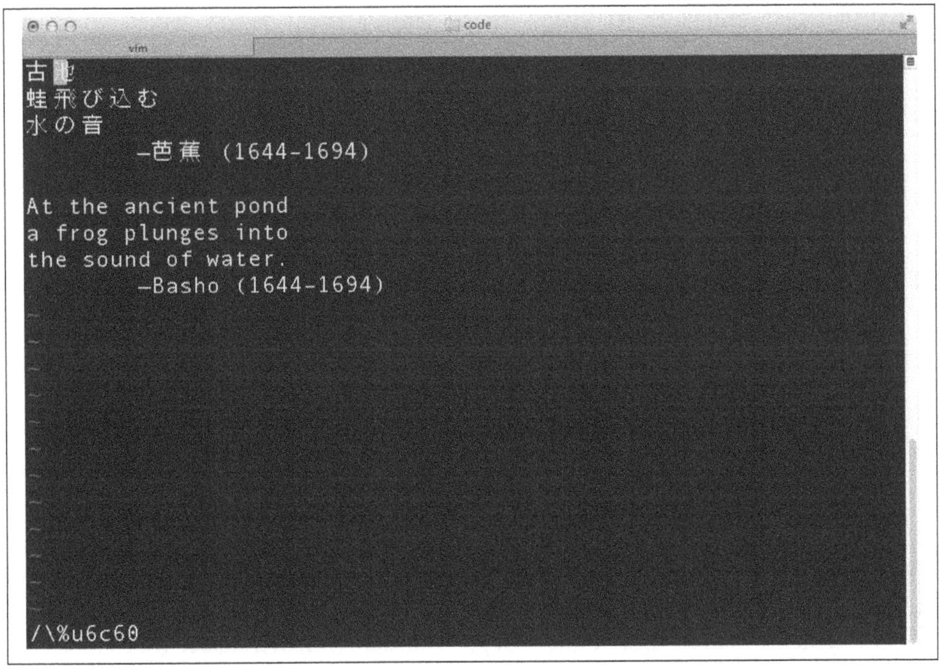

Figure 6-3. Matching U+6c60 in Vim

Matching Characters with Octal Numbers

You can also match characters using an octal (base 8) number, which uses the digits 0 to 7. In regex, this is done with three digits, preceded by a slash (\).

For example, the following octal number:

    \351

is the same as:

    \u00e9

Experiment with it in Regexpal with the Voltaire text. \351 matches *é*, with a little less typing.

Matching Unicode Character Properties

In some implementations, such as Perl, you can match on Unicode character properties. The properties include characteristics like whether the character is a letter, number, or punctuation mark.

I'll now introduce you to *ack*, a command-line tool written in Perl that acts a lot like *grep* (see *http://betterthangrep.com*). It won't come on your system; you have to download and install it yourself (see "Technical Notes" (page 73)).

We'll use *ack* on an excerpt from Friederich Schiller's "An die Freude," composed in 1785 (German, if you can't tell):

```
An die Freude.

Freude, schöner Götterfunken,
Tochter aus Elisium,
Wir betreten feuertrunken
Himmlische, dein Heiligthum.
Deine Zauber binden wieder,
was der Mode Schwerd getheilt;
Bettler werden Fürstenbrüder,
wo dein sanfter Flügel weilt.

Seid umschlungen, Millionen!
Diesen Kuß der ganzen Welt!
Brüder, überm Sternenzelt
muß ein lieber Vater wohnen.
```

There are a few interesting characters in this excerpt, beyond ASCII's small realm. We'll look at the text of this poem through properties. (If you would like a translation of this poem fragment, you can drop it into Google Translate (*http://translate.google.com*).

Using *ack* on a command line, you can specify that you want to see all the characters whose property is Letter (L):

```
ack '\pL' schiller.txt
```

This will show you all the letters highlighted. For lowercase letters, use *Ll*, surrounded by braces:

```
ack '\p{Ll}' schiller.txt
```

You must add the braces. For uppercase, it's *Lu*:

```
ack '\p{Lu}' schiller.txt
```

To specify characters that do *not* match a property, we use uppercase *P*:

```
ack '\PL' schiller.txt
```

This highlights characters that are not letters.

The following finds those that are not lowercase letters:

```
ack '\P{Ll}' schiller.txt
```

And this highlights the ones that are not uppercase:

```
ack '\P{Lu}' schiller.txt
```

You can also do this in yet another browser-based regex tester, *http://regex.larsolavtor vik.com*. Figure 6-4 shows the Schiller text with its lowercase letters highlighted using the lowercase property

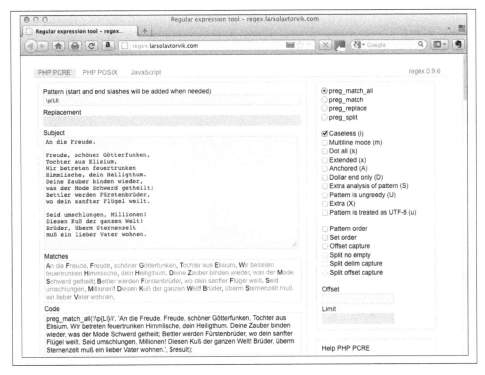

Figure 6-4. Characters with the lowercase letter property

Table 6-2 lists character property names for use with \p{*property*} or \P{*property*} (see pcresyntax(3) at *http://www.pcre.org/pcre.txt*). You can also match human languages with properties; see Table A-8.

Table 6-2. Character properties

Property	Description
C	Other
Cc	Control

Property	Description
Cf	Format
Cn	Unassigned
Co	Private use
Cs	Surrogate
L	Letter
Ll	Lowercase letter
Lm	Modifier letter
Lo	Other letter
Lt	Title case letter
Lu	Uppercase letter
L&	Ll, Lu, or Lt
M	Mark
Mc	Spacing mark
Me	Enclosing mark
Mn	Non-spacing mark
N	Number
Nd	Decimal number
Nl	Letter number
No	Other number
P	Punctuation
Pc	Connector punctuation
Pd	Dash punctuation
Pe	Close punctuation
Pf	Final punctuation
Pi	Initial punctuation
Po	Other punctuation
Ps	Open punctuation
S	Symbol
Sc	Currency symbol
Sk	Modifier symbol
Sm	Mathematical symbol
So	Other symbol
Z	Separator
Zl	Line separator
Zp	Paragraph separator
Zs	Space separator

Matching Control Characters

How do you match control characters? It's not all that common that you will search for control characters in text, but it's a good thing to know. In the example repository or archive, you'll find the file *ascii.txt*, which is a 128-line file that contains all the ASCII characters in it, each on separate line (hence the 128 lines). When you perform a search on the file, it will usually return a single line if it finds a match. This file is good for testing and general fun.

If you search for strings or control characters in *ascii.txt* with *grep* or *ack*, they may interpret the file as a binary file. If so, when you run a script on it, either tool may simply report "Binary file ascii.txt matches" when it finds a match. That's all.

In regular expressions, you can specify a control character like this:

```
\cx
```

where *x* is the control character you want to match.

Let's say, for example, you wanted to find a null character in a file. You can use Perl to do that with the following command:

```
perl -n -e 'print if /\c@/' ascii.txt
```

Provided that you've got Perl on your system and it's running properly, you will get this result:

```
0. Null
```

The reason why is that there is a null character on that line, even though you can't see the character in the result.

If you open *ascii.txt* with an editor other than *vim*, it will likely remove the control characters from the file, so I suggest you don't do it.

You can also use \0 to find a null character. Try this, too:

```
perl -n -e 'print if /\0/' ascii.txt
```

Pressing on, you can find the bell (BEL) character using:

```
perl -n -e 'print if /\cG/' ascii.txt
```

It will return the line:

```
7. Bell
```

Or you can use the shorthand:

```
perl -n -e 'print if /\a/' ascii.txt
```

To find the escape character, use:

```
perl -n -e 'print if /\c[/' ascii.txt
```

which gives you:

```
27. Escape
```

Or do it with a shorthand:

```
perl -n -e 'print if /\e/' ascii.txt
```

How about a backspace character? Try:

```
perl -n -e 'print if /\cH/' ascii.txt
```

which spits back:

```
8. Backspace
```

You can also find a backspace using a bracketed expression:

```
perl -n -e 'print if /[\b]/' ascii.txt
```

Without the brackets, how would \b be interpreted? That's right, as a word boundary, as you learned in Chapter 2. The brackets change the way the \b is understood by the processor. In this case, Perl sees it as a backspace character.

Table 6-3 lists the ways we matched characters in this chapter.

Table 6-3. Matching Unicode and other characters

Code	Description
\u*xxxx*	Unicode (four places)
xxx	Unicode (two places)
	Unicode (four places)
	Unicode (two places)
\000	Octal (base 8)
\cx	Control character
\0	Null
\a	Bell
\e	Escape
\[\b\]	Backspace

That wraps things up for this chapter. In the next, you'll learn more about quantifiers.

What You Learned in Chapter 6

- How to match any Unicode character with \u*xxxx* or *xxx*
- How to match any Unicode character inside of *vim* using \%*xxx*, \%X*xx*, \%u*xxxx*, or \%U*xxxx*
- How to match characters in the range 0–255 using octal format with \000
- How to use Unicode character properties with \p{*x*}
- How to match control characters with \e or \cH
- More on how to use Perl on the command line (more Perl one-liners)

Technical Notes

- I entered control characters in *ascii.txt* using *vim* (*http://www.vim.org*). In *vim*, you can use Ctrl+V followed by the appropriate control sequence for the character, such as Ctrl+C for the end-of-text character. I also used Ctrl+V followed by *x* and the two-digit hexadecimal code for the character. You can also use digraphs to enter control codes; in *vim* enter :digraph to see the possible codes. To enter a digraph, use Ctrl+K while in Insert mode, followed by a two-character digraph (for example, *NU* for null).

- RegexHero (*http://regexhero.net/tester*) is a .NET regex implementation in a browser written by Steve Wortham. This one is for pay, but you can test it out for free, and if you like it, the prices are reasonable (you can buy it at a standard or a professional level).

- *vim* (*http://www.vim.org*) is an evolution of the *vi* editor that was created by Bill Joy in 1976. The *vim* editor was developed primarily by Bram Moolenaar. It seems archaic to the uninitiated, but as I've mentioned, it is incredibly powerful.

- The *ack* tool (*http://betterthangrep.com*) is written in Perl. It acts like *grep* and has many of its command line options, but it outperforms *grep* in many ways. For example, it uses Perl regular expressions instead of basic regular expressions like *grep* (without *-E*). For installation instructions, see *http://betterthangrep.com/install/*. I used the specific instructions under "Install the ack executable." I didn't use *curl* but just downloaded *ack* with the link provided and then copied the script into */usr/bin* on both my Mac and a PC running Cygwin (*http://www.cygwin.com*) in Windows 7.

CHAPTER 7

Quantifiers

You have already seen some quantifiers at work earlier in this book, but here I'll talk about them in more detail.

For our example this time, we'll use a Mac desktop application called Reggy (Figure 7-1), as we did in Chapter 5. Uncheck *Match All* at the bottom to start.

If you are not on a Mac, you can try these examples in one of the applications you've seen earlier in the book. Paste the right triangle of digits from the *triangle.txt*. The file is in the archive of examples.

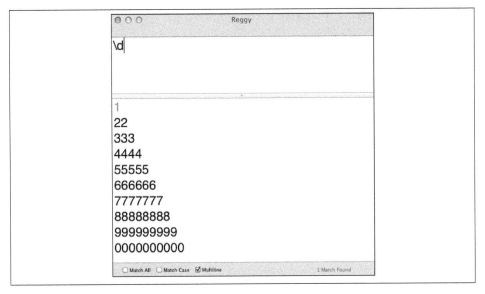

Figure 7-1. Reggy application

Greedy, Lazy, and Possessive

I'm not talking about your teenager here. I'm talking about quantifiers. These adjectives may not sound like good character qualities, but they are interesting features of quantifiers that you need to understand if you want to use regular expressions with skill.

Quantifiers are, by themselves, greedy. A greedy quantifier first tries to match the whole string. It grabs as much as it can, the whole input, trying to make a match. If the first attempt to match the whole string goes awry, it backs up one character and tries again. This is called *backtracking*. It keeps backing up one character at a time until it finds a match or runs out of characters to try. It also keeps track of what it is doing, so it puts the most load on resources compared with the next two approaches. It takes a mouthful, then spits back a little at a time, chewing on what it just ate. You get the idea.

A lazy (sometimes called *reluctant*) quantifier takes a different tack. It starts at the beginning of the target, trying to find a match. It looks at the string one character at a time, trying to find what it is looking for. At last, it will attempt to match the whole string. To get a quantifier to be lazy, you have to append a question mark (?) to the regular quantifier. It chews one nibble at a time.

A possessive quantifier grabs the whole target and then tries to find a match, but it makes only one attempt. It does not do any backtracking. A possessive quantifier appends a plus sign (+) to the regular quantifier. It doesn't chew; it just swallows, then wonders what it just ate. I'll demonstrate each of these in the pages that follow.

Matching with *, +, and ?

If you have the triangle of digits in Reggy, you can now begin testing. First we'll use the Kleene star, named for the man credited as the inventor of regular expressions, Stephen Kleene. If you use the star or asterisk following a dot like this:

    .*

it would match, being greedy, all the characters (digits) in the subject text. As you know from earlier reading, . * matches any character zero or more times. All the digits in the lower box should be highlighted by changing color. Of the Kleene star, an early manual said:

> A regular expression followed by "*" [Kleene star] is a regular expression which matches any number (including zero) of adjacent occurrences of the text matched by the regular expression.

Now try:

9*

and the row of nines near the bottom should be highlighted. Now:

9.*

lights up the row of nines and the row of zeros below it. Because *Multiline* is checked (at the bottom of the application window), the dot will match the newline character between the rows; normally, it would not.

To match one or more 9s, try:

9+

How is that different? You can't really tell because there are nine 9s in the subject text. The main difference is that + is looking for at least one 9, but * is looking for zero or more.

To match zero or one time (optional), use:

9?

This will match the first occurrence of 9 only. That 9 is considered optional, so because it does exist in the subject text, it is matched and highlighted. If you do this:

99?

then both the first and second 9 are matched.

Table 7-1 lists the basic quantifiers and some of the possibilities that they have. These quantifiers are by default *greedy*, meaning that they match as many characters as they possibly can on the first attempt.

Table 7-1. Basic quantifiers

Syntax	Description
?	Zero or one (optional)
+	One or more
*	Zero or more

Matching a Specific Number of Times

When you use braces or squiggly brackets, you can match a pattern a specific number of times in a range. Unmodified, these are greedy quantifiers. For example:

7{1}

will match the first occurrence of 7. If you wanted to match one *or more* occurrences of the number 7, all you have to do is add a comma:

```
7{1,}
```

You've probably realized that both:

```
7+
```

and:

```
7{1,}
```

are essentially the same thing, and that:

```
7*
```

and:

```
7{0,}
```

are likewise the same. In addition:

```
7?
```

is the same as:

```
7{0,1}
```

To find a range of matches, that is, to match *m* to *n* times:

```
7{3,5}
```

This will match three, four, or five occurrences of 7.

So to review, the squiggly bracket or range syntax is the most flexible and precise quantifier. Table 7-2 summarizes these features.

Table 7-2. Summary of range syntax

Syntax	Description
{*n*}	Match *n* times exactly
{*n,*}	Match *n* or more times
{*m,n*}	Match *m* to *n* times
{0,1}	Same as ? (zero or one)
{1,0}	Same as + (one or more)
{0,}	Same as \ * (zero or more)

Lazy Quantifiers

Now let's set aside greediness and get lazy. The easiest way for you to understand this is by seeing it in action. In Reggy (making sure *Match All* is unchecked), try to match zero or one 5 using a single question mark (?):

```
5?
```

The first 5 is highlighted. Add an additional ? to make the quantifier lazy:

    5??

Now it doesn't appear to match anything. The reason why is that the pattern is being lazy, that is, it's not even forced to match that first 5. By nature, the *lazy* match matches as few characters as it can get away with. It's a slacker.

Try this zero or more times:

    5*?

and it won't match anything either, because you gave it the option to match a minimum of zero times, and that's what it does.

Try it again matching one or more times, à la lazy:

    5+?

And there you go. Lazy just got off the couch and matched one 5. That's all it had to do to keep its day job.

Things get a bit more interesting as you apply *m,n* matching. Try this:

    5{2,5}?

Only two 5s are matched, not all five of them, as a greedy match would.

Table 7-3 lists the lazy quantifiers. When is lazy matching useful? You can use lazy matching when you want to match the bare minimum of characters, not the maximum possible.

Table 7-3. Lazy quantifiers

Syntax	Description
??	Lazy zero or one (optional)
+?	Lazy one or more
*?	Lazy zero or more
{n}?	Lazy n
{n,}?	Lazy n or more
{m,n}?	Lazy m,n

Possessive Quantifiers

A possessive match is like a greedy match, it grabs as much as it can get away with. But unlike a greedy match: It does not backtrack. It does not give up anything it finds. It is selfish. That is why it is called *possessive*. Arms folded firmly, it doesn't give up any ground. But the good thing about possessive quantifiers is that they are faster, because they don't do any backtracking, and they also fail in a hurry.

The truth is, you can hardly tell the difference between greedy, lazy, and possessive matches with the examples in this book. But as you gain more experience, and performance tuning becomes important, you'll want to be aware of these differences.

To make sense of this, first we'll try matching the zeroes with a leading zero, then with a trailing zero. In Reggy, make sure *Match All* is checked, and enter this expression with a leading zero:

```
0.*+
```

What happened? All the zeroes are highlighted. There was a match. The possessive match appears to do the same thing as a greedy match, with one subtle difference: There is no backtracking. You can now prove it. Enter this with a trailing zero:

```
.*+0
```

No match. The reason why is there was no backtracking. It gobbled up the entire input and never looked back. It wasted its inheritance with riotous living. It can't find the trailing zero. It doesn't know where to look. If you remove the plus sign, it would find all the zeroes as it goes back to a greedy match:

```
.*0
```

You might want to use a possessive quantifier when you are aware of what is in your text, you know where you will find matches. You don't care if it grabs with gusto. A possessive match can help you match with improved performance. Table 7-4 shows the possessive quantifiers.

Table 7-4. Possessive quantifiers

Syntax	Description
?+	Possessive zero or one (optional)
++	Possessive one or more
*+	Possessive zero or more
{n}+	Possessive n
{n,}+	Possessive n or more
{m,n}+	Possessive m,n

You'll be introduced to lookarounds in the next chapter.

What You Learned in Chapter 7

- The differences between greedy, lazy, and possessive matching
- How to match one or more (+)
- How to match optionally (zero or one, ?)
- How to match zero or one (*)
- How to use {*m*,*n*} quantifiers
- How to use greedy, lazy (reluctant), and possessive quantifiers.

Technical Notes

The quote comes from Ken Thompson, *QED Text Editor* (Murray Hill, NJ, Bell Labs, 1970) p. 3 (see *http://cm.bell-labs.com/cm/cs/who/dmr/qedman.pdf*).

CHAPTER 8

Lookarounds

Lookarounds are non-capturing groups that match patterns based on what they find either in front of or behind a pattern. Lookarounds are also considered *zero-width assertions*.

Lookarounds include:

- Positive lookaheads
- Negative lookaheads
- Positive lookbehinds
- Negative lookbehinds

In this chapter, I'll show you how each of these works. We'll start out using RegExr on the desktop and then move on to Perl and *ack* (*grep* doesn't know about lookarounds). Our text is still Coleridge's well-worn poem.

Positive Lookaheads

Suppose you want to find every occurrence of the word *ancyent* that is followed by *marinere* (I use the archaic spellings because that is what is found in the file). To do this, we could use a positive lookahead.

First let's try it in RegExr desktop. The following case-insentitive pattern goes in the text box at the top:

```
(?i)ancyent (?=marinere)
```

You can also specify case-insensitivity with RegExr by simply checking the box next to *ignoreCase*, but both methods work.

Because you use the case-insensitive option (?i), you don't need to worry about what case you use in your pattern. You are looking for every line that has the word *ancyent* followed hard by *marinere*. The results will be highlighted in the text area below the pattern area (see Figure 8-1); however, only the first part of the pattern will be highlighted (*ancyent*), not the lookahead pattern (*Marinere*).

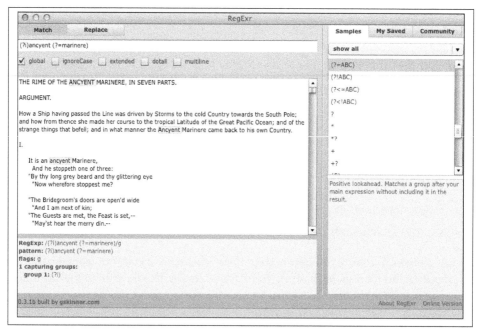

Figure 8-1. Positive lookahead in RegExr

Let's now use Perl to do a positive lookahead. You can form the command like so:

```
perl -ne 'print if /(?i)ancyent (?=marinere)/' rime.txt
```

and the output should look like this:

```
THE RIME OF THE ANCYENT MARINERE, IN SEVEN PARTS.
How a Ship having passed the Line was driven by Storms to the cold Country
towards the South Pole; and how from thence she made her course to the tropical
Latitude of the Great Pacific Ocean; and of the strange things that befell; and
```

```
in what manner the Ancyent Marinere came back to his own Country.
    It is an ancyent Marinere,
    "God save thee, ancyent Marinere!
    "I fear thee, ancyent Marinere!
```

There are five lines in the poem where the word *ancyent* shows up right before the word *marinere*. What if we just wanted to check if the word following *ancyent* started with the letter *m*, either in upper- or lowercase? We could do it this way:

```
perl -ne 'print if /(?i)ancyent (?=m)/' rime.txt
```

In addition to `Marinere`, you would get `man` and `Man`:

```
And thus spake on that ancyent man,
And thus spake on that ancyent Man,
```

ack also can do lookarounds as it is written in Perl. The command-line interface for *ack* is very similar to *grep*.

Try this:

```
ack '(?i)ancyent (?=ma)' rime.txt
```

and you'll see highlighted results, as shown in Figure 8-2.

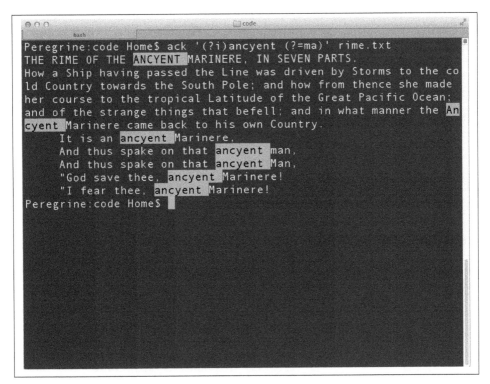

Figure 8-2. Positive lookahead with ack in Terminal

With *ack*, you can specify case-insensitivity with the command-line option *-i*, rather than with the embedded option (?i):

```
ack -i 'ancyent (?=ma)' rime.txt
```

I'll throw something in here for good measure. If you want to add line numbers to *ack's* output, you can do several things. You can add the *-H* option:

```
ack -Hi 'ancyent (?=ma)' rime.txt
```

Or you could add this code with the *--output* option:

```
ack -i --output '$.:$_' 'ancyent (?=ma)' rime.txt
```

This is a bit of a hack, and turns off highlighting, but it works.

Negative Lookaheads

The flip side of a positive lookahead is a negative lookahead. This means that as you try to match a pattern, you *won't* find a given lookahead pattern. A negative lookahead is formed like this:

```
(?i)ancyent (?!marinere)
```

Only one character changed: The equals sign (=) in the positive lookahead became an exclamation point (!) in the negative lookahead. Figure 8-3 shows you this negative lookahead in Opera.

In Perl, we could do a negative lookahead this way:

```
perl -ne 'print if /(?i)ancyent (?!marinere)/' rime.txt
```

and this is what we would get back:

```
And thus spake on that ancyent man,
And thus spake on that ancyent Man,
```

In *ack*, the same results could be produced with:

```
ack -i 'ancyent (?!marinere)' rime.txt
```

Positive Lookbehinds

A positive lookbehind looks to the left, in the opposite direction as a lookahead. The syntax is:

```
(?i)(?<=ancyent) marinere
```

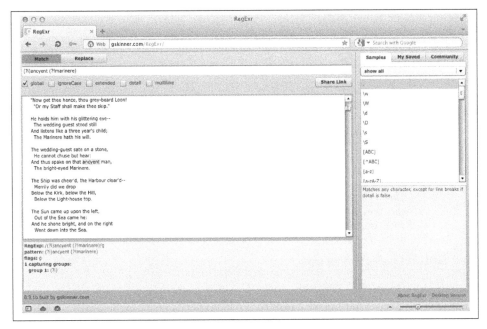

Figure 8-3. Negative lookahead with RegExr in Opera

The positive lookbehind throws in a less-than sign (<), reminding you which direction lookbehind is. Try this in RegExr and see what the difference is. Instead of *ancyent* being highlighted, *marinere* is. Why? Because the positive lookbehind is a condition of the match and is not included or consumed in the match results.

Do it like so in Perl:

```
perl -ne 'print if /(?i)(?<=ancyent) marinere/' rime.txt
```

And like this with *ack*:

```
ack -i '(?<=ancyent) marinere' rime.txt
```

Negative Lookbehinds

Finally, there is the negative lookbehind. And how do you think this one works?

It is looking to see if a pattern does *not* show up behind in the left-to-right stream of text. Again, it adds a less-than sign (<), reminding you which direction lookbehind is.

Do this in RegExr and see the results:

```
(?i)(?<!ancyent) marinere
```

Scroll down to see what you got.

Then try it in Perl:

```
perl -ne 'print if /(?i)(?<!ancyent) marinere/' rime.txt
```

What you should see is this, with no sign of *ancyent* anywhere:

```
The Marinere hath his will.
The bright-eyed Marinere.
The bright-eyed Marinere.
The Marineres gave it biscuit-worms,
  Came to the Marinere's hollo!
  Came to the Marinere's hollo!
The Marineres all 'gan work the ropes,
The Marineres all return'd to work
The Marineres all 'gan pull the ropes,
  "When the Marinere's trance is abated."
He loves to talk with Marineres
The Marinere, whose eye is bright,
```

And, lastly, do it this way in *ack*:

```
ack -i '(?<!ancyent) marinere' rime.txt
```

That wraps up our brief introduction to for lookaheads and lookbehinds, a powerful feature of modern regular expressions.

In the next chapter, you'll see a full example of how to mark up a document with HTML5 using *sed* and Perl.

What You Learned in Chapter 8

- How to do positive and negative lookaheads
- How to do both positive and negative lookbehinds

Technical Notes

See also pages 59 through 66 of *Mastering Regular Expressions, Third Edition* (*http:// shop.oreilly.com/product/9780596528126.do*).

CHAPTER 9

Marking Up a Document with HTML

This chapter will take you step by step through the process of marking up plain-text documents with HTML5 using regular expressions, concluding what we started early in the book.

Now, if it were me, I'd use AsciiDoc to do this work. But for our purposes here, we'll pretend that there is no such thing as AsciiDoc (what a shame). We'll plod along using a few tools we have at hand—namely, *sed* and Perl—and our own ingenuity.

For our text we'll still use Coleridge's poem in *rime.txt*.

 The scripts in this chapter work well with *rime.txt* because you understand the structure of that file. These scripts will give you less predictable results when used on arbitrary text files; however, they give you a starting point for handling text structures in more complex files.

Matching Tags

Before we start adding markup to the poem, let's talk about how to match either HTML or XML tags. There are a variety of ways to match a tag, either start-tags (e.g., <html>) or end-tags (e.g., </html>), but I have found the one that follows to be reliable. It will match start-tags, with or without attributes:

```
<[_a-zA-Z][^>]*>
```

Here is what it does:

- The first character is a left angle bracket (<).
- Elements can begin with an underscore character (_) in XML or a letter in the ASCII range, in either upper- or lowercase (see "Technical Notes" (page 101)).

- Following the start character, the name can be followed by zero or more characters, any character other than a right angle bracket (>).

- The expression ends with a right angle bracket.

Try this with *grep*. Match it against a sample DITA file in the archive, *lorem.dita*:

```
grep -Eo '<[_a-zA-Z][^>]*>' lorem.dita
```

yields this answer:

```
<topic id="lorem">
<title>
<body>
<p>
<p>
<ul>
<li>
<li>
<li>
<p>
<p>
```

To match both start- and end-tags, simply add a forward slash followed by a question mark. The question mark makes the forward slash optional:

```
</?[_a-zA-Z][^>]*>
```

I'm sticking with start-tags only here. To refine the output, I often pipe in a few other tools to make it prettier:

```
grep -Eo '<[_a-zA-Z][^>]*>' lorem.dita | sort | uniq | sed 's/^<//;s/ id=\".*
\"//;s/>
    $//'
```

This gives you a list of sorted XML tag names:

```
body
li
p
p
title
topic
ul
```

I'll take this a step further in the next and final chapter. The following sections will take you through some of the steps you have learned before, but with a few new twists.

Transforming Plain Text with *sed*

Let's add some markup to the top of the text in *rime.txt*. We can do this with the insert command (i\). In the directory where the *rime.txt* file is located, enter the following at a shell prompt:

```
sed '1 i\
<!DOCTYPE html>\
<html lang="en">\
<head>\
<title>The Rime of the Ancyent Marinere (1798)</title>\
<meta charset="utf-8"/>\
</head>\
<body>\

q' rime.txt
```

After you press Enter or Return, your output should look like the following, with the tags at the top:

```
<!DOCTYPE html>
<html lang="en">
<head>
<title>The Rime of the Ancyent Marinere (1798)</title>
<meta charset="utf-8"/>
</head>
<body>
THE RIME OF THE ANCYENT MARINERE, IN SEVEN PARTS.
```

The command you just entered did not actually change the file—it only produced an output to your screen. I'll show you how to write your changes to a file later.

Substitution with sed

In the next example, *sed* finds the first line of the file and captures the entire line in a capturing group using escaped parentheses \(and \). *sed* needs to escape the parentheses used to capture a group unless you use the -E option (more on this in a moment). The beginning of the line is demarcated with \^, and the end of the line with a $. The backreference \1 pulls the captured text into the content of the *title* element, indented with one space.

Run the command that follows:

```
sed '1s/^\(.*\)$/ <title>\1<\/title>/;q' rime.txt
```

The resulting line looks like this:

```
<title>THE RIME OF THE ANCYENT MARINERE, IN SEVEN PARTS.</title>
```

Now try it this way:

```
sed -E '1s/^(.*)$/<!DOCTYPE html>\
<html lang="en">\
<head>\
 <title>\1<\/title>\
<\/head>\
<body>\
<h1>\1<\/h1>\
/;q' rime.txt
```

Let's talk about it:

- The *-E* options tells *sed* to use extended regular expressions or EREs (so you don't have to escape the parentheses, etc.).
- Using a substitute (*s*) command, grab line 1 in a capturing group (\^(.*)$) so you can reuse the text with \1.
- Create HTML tags and escape newlines with \.
- Insert the captured text in the *title* and *h1* tags using \1.
- Quit at this point (q) to stop printing the rest of the poem to the screen.

The correct result is:

```
<!DOCTYPE html>
<html lang="en">
<head>
 <title>THE RIME OF THE ANCYENT MARINERE, IN SEVEN PARTS.</title>
</head>
<body>
<h1>THE RIME OF THE ANCYENT MARINERE, IN SEVEN PARTS.</h1>
```

Handling Roman Numerals with *sed*

The poem is divided into seven sections, with each section introduced with a Roman numeral. There is also an "ARGUMENT" heading. The following line will use *sed* to capture that heading and those Roman numerals and surround them in *h2* tags:

```
sed -En 's/^(ARGUMENT\.|I{0,3}V?I{0,2}\.)$/<h2>\1<\/h2>/p' rime.txt
```

and here is what you'll see:

```
<h2>ARGUMENT\.</h2>
<h2>I.</h2>
<h2>II.</h2>
<h2>III.</h2>
<h2>IV.</h2>
<h2>V.</h2>
<h2>VI.</h2>
<h2>VII.</h2>
```

Following is a description of this previous *sed* command:

- The *-E* option gives you extended regular expressions, and the *-n* option suppresses the printing of each line, which is *sed*'s default behavior.
- The substitute (*s*) command captures the heading and the seven uppercase Roman numerals, each on separate lines and followed by a period, in the range I through VII.
- The *s* command then takes each line of captured text and nestles it in an *h2* element.

- The *p* flag at the end of the substitution prints the result to the screen.

Handling a Specific Paragraph with *sed*

Next, this line finds a paragraph on line 5:

```
sed -En '5s/^([A-Z].*)$/<p>\1<\/p>/p' rime.txt
```

and places that paragraph in a *p* tag:

```
<p>How a Ship having passed the Line was driven by Storms to the cold Country
    towards the South Pole; and how from thence she made her course to the
    tropical Latitude of the Great Pacific Ocean; and of the strange things
    that befell; and in what manner the Ancyent Marinere came back to his
    own Country.<p>
```

I know this looks like we are moving inchmeal at the moment, but hang on and I'll bring it all together in a page or two.

Handling the Lines of the Poem with *sed*

Next we'll mark up the lines of the poem with:

```
sed -E '9s/^[ ]*(.*)/  <p>\1<br\/>/;10,832s/^([ ]{5,7}.*)/\1<br\/>/;
    833s/^(.*)/\1<\/p>/' rime.txt
```

These *sed* substitutions depend on line numbers to get their little jobs done. This wouldn't work with a generalized case, but it works quite well when you know exactly what you are dealing with.

- On line 9, the first line of verse, the *s* command grabs the line and, after prepending a few spaces, it inserts a *p* start-tag and appends a *br* (break) tag at the end of the line.
- Between lines 10 and 832, every line that begins with between 5 to 7 spaces gets a *br* appended to it.
- On line 833, the last line of the poem, instead of a *br*, the *s* appends a *p* end-tag.

A sample of the resulting markup is here:

```
<p>It is an ancyent Marinere,<br/>
    And he stoppeth one of three:<br/>
  "By thy long grey beard and thy glittering eye<br/>
    "Now wherefore stoppest me?<br/>

  "The Bridegroom's doors are open'd wide<br/>
    "And I am next of kin;<br/>
  "The Guests are met, the Feast is set,--<br/>
    "May'st hear the merry din.--<br/>
```

You should also replace the blank lines with a *br*, to keep the verses separated:

```
sed -E 's/^$/<br\/>/' rime.txt
```

See what you just did:

```
      He prayeth best who loveth best,
        All things both great and small:
      For the dear God, who loveth us,
        He made and loveth all.
<br/>
      The Marinere, whose eye is bright,
        Whose beard with age is hoar,
      Is gone; and now the wedding-guest
        Turn'd from the bridegroom's door.
<br/>
      He went, like one that hath been stunn'd
        And is of sense forlorn:
      A sadder and a wiser man
        He rose the morrow morn.
```

I have found that I can play with this kind of thing endlessly, getting the tags and space just right. I encourage you to do so yourself.

Appending Tags

Now we'll append some tags to the end of the poem. With the append command (a\), the $ finds the end (the last line) of the file, and appends (a\) the *body* and *html* end-tags after the last line:

```
sed '$ a\
<\/body>\
<\/html>\
' rime.txt
```

Here's how the end of the file will look now:

```
      He went, like one that hath been stunn'd
        And is of sense forlorn:
      A sadder and a wiser man
        He rose the morrow morn.
</body>
</html>
```

Enough *sed*.

What if you wanted to do all of these changes at the same time? You know what to do. You've already done it. You just have to put all these commands in a file and use the *-f* option with *sed*.

Using a Command File with *sed*

This example shows the file *html.sed*, which collects all the previous *sed* commands into one file, plus a command or two more. We'll use this file of commands to transform *rime.txt* to HTML using *sed*. The numbered callouts in the example will guide you through what is happening in the *sed* script:

```
#!/usr/bin/sed ❶

1s/^(.*)$/<!DOCTYPE html>\ ❷
<html lang="en">\
<head>\
 <title>\1</title>\
<\/head>\
<body>\
<h1>\1<\/h1>\
/

s/^(ARGUMENT|I{0,3}V?I{0,2})\.$/<h2>\1<\/h2>/ ❸
5s/^([A-Z].*)$/<p>\1<\/p>/ ❹
9s/^[ ]*(.*)/  <p>\1<br\/>/ ❺
10,832s/^([ ]{5,7}.*)/\1<br\/>/ ❻
833s/^(.*)/\1<\/p>/ ❼
13,$s/^$/<br\/>/ ❽
$ a\ ❾
<\/body>\
<\/html>\
```

❶   The first line is called the *shebang* line, a hint to the shell of where the executable (*sed*) is located.

❷   At line 1, substitute (*s*) the line with the tags that follow. The backslash (\) indicates that the text you want to add continues on the next line so a newline is inserted. Insert the title of the poem from line 1 with \1, as the content of *title* and *h1* elements.

❸   Surround headings and Roman numerals with *h2* tags.

❹   On line 5, enclose the introductory paragraph in a *p* element.

❺   On line 9, prepend a *p* start-tag and add a *br* at the end of the line.

❻   Between line 9 and 832, add a *br* at the end of each line that begins with a certain number of spaces.

❼   At the end of the poem, append a *p* end-tag.

❽   After line 13, replace each blank line with a break (*br*).

❾   Appends a few tags at the end ($) of the document.

To apply this command file to *rime.txt*, enter this line, followed by Enter or Return:

```
sed -E -f html.sed rime.txt
```

To redirect the output to a file:

```
sed -E -f html.sed rime.txt &gt; rime.html
```

Open *rime.html* in a browser to see what you have created (see Figure 9-1).

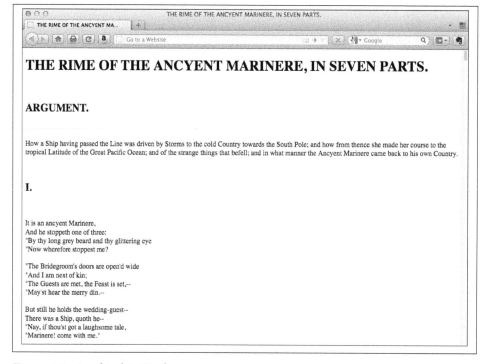

Figure 9-1. rime.html in Firefox

Transforming Plain Text with Perl

I'll now show you how to mark up a file with HTML using Perl. First, like with *sed*, I'll give you a series of one-liners; then I'll show those same commands in a file.

> This book introduces you to only the rudiments of the Perl language, and how to get started using it. It is not a Perl tutorial or manual, but I hope to pique your interest in Perl and show you a few possibilities. A good place to get started with Perl is at the Learning Perl website found at *http://learn.perl.org/*, which also includes instructions on how to install it.

If the current line ($.) is line 1, assign the whole line ($_) to the *$title* variable and print *$title*.

```
perl -ne 'if ($. == 1) {chomp($title = $_); print "<h1>" . $title . "</h1>" .
"\n";};'
    rime.txt
```

If all goes well, the result should be:

```
<h1>THE RIME OF THE ANCYENT MARINERE, IN SEVEN PARTS.</h1>
```

Here is an explanation for the Perl command :

- Test if you are on line 1 with $.

- Chomp the line ($_) and assign the string to the $title variable. When you chomp the line with the *chomp* function, it removes the trailing newline from the string.

- Print $title in an *h1* element, followed by a newline (\n).

 For more information on Perl's built-in variables, such as $., enter the command perldoc -v $. at a prompt (*perldoc* normally is installed when you install Perl). If this doesn't work, see "Technical Notes" (page 101).

To prepend some markup to the top of the file, including that *h1* tag, use this:

```
perl -ne 'if ($. == 1) {chomp($title = $_)};
print "<!DOCTYPE html>\
<html xmlns=\"http://www.w3.org/1999/xhtml\">\
  <head>\
    <title>$title</title>\
    <meta charset=\"utf-8\"/>\
  </head>\
<body>\
<h1>$title</h1>\n" if $. == 1; exit' rime.txt
```

and you'll get the following output:

```
<!DOCTYPE html>
<html xmlns="http://www.w3.org/1999/xhtml">
  <head>
    <title>THE RIME OF THE ANCYENT MARINERE, IN SEVEN PARTS.</title>
    <meta charset=\"utf-8\"/>
  </head>
<body>
<h1>THE RIME OF THE ANCYENT MARINERE, IN SEVEN PARTS.</h1>
```

The *print* function prints the tags that follow, and each line (except the last), is followed by a \, which enters a newline into the output. The $title variable is expanded within the *title* and *h1* elements.

Handling Roman Numerals with Perl

To tag up the heading and those Roman numeral section breaks, use:

```
perl -ne 'print if s/^(ARGUMENT\.|I{0,3}V?I{0,2}\.)$/<h2>\1<\/h2>/;' rime.txt
```

This is the output:

```
<h2>ARGUMENT.</h2>
<h2>I.</h2>
<h2>II.</h2>
<h2>III.</h2>
<h2>IV.</h2>
<h2>V.</h2>
<h2>VI.</h2>
<h2>VII.</h2>
```

The substitute (*s*) command captures the *ARGUMENT* heading and those seven uppercase Roman numerals, each on separate lines and followed by a period, in the range I through VII. Then it encloses the captured text in an *h2* tag.

Handling a Specific Paragraph with Perl

Use this code to enclose the introductory paragraph in a *p* element, if the line number is equal to 5:

```
perl -ne 'if ($. == 5) {s/^([A-Z].*)$/<p>$1<\/p>/;print;}' rime.txt
```

You should see this:

```
<p>How a Ship having passed the Line was driven by Storms to the cold Country
    towards the South Pole; and how from thence she made her course to the
    tropical Latitude of the Great Pacific Ocean; and of the strange things
    that befell; and in what manner the Ancyent Marinere came back to his
    own Country.</p>
```

Handling the Lines of the Poem with Perl

The following command places a *p* start-tag at the beginning of the first line of the poem, and a *br* tag after the end of that line:

```
perl -ne 'if ($. == 9) {s/^[ ]*(.*)/  <p>$1<br\/>/;print;}' rime.txt
```

It gives you:

```
<p>It is an ancyent Marinere,<br/>
```

Next, between lines 10 and 832, this bit of Perl puts a *br* at the end of each line of the poem:

```
perl -ne 'if (10..832) { s/^([ ]{5,7}.*)/$1<br\/>/; print;}' rime.txt
```

A sample of what you will see:

```
Farewell, farewell! but this I tell<br/>
  To thee, thou wedding-guest!<br/>
He prayeth well who loveth well<br/>
  Both man and bird and beast.<br/>
```

Add a *p* end-tag to the end of the last line of the poem:

```
perl -ne 'if ($. == 833) {s/^(.*)/$1<\/p>/; print;}' rime.txt
```

It shows:

```
He rose the morrow morn.</p>
```

Replace blank lines at the end of each line with a *br* tag:

```
perl -ne 'if (9..eof) {s/^$/<br\/>/; print;}' rime.txt
```

to yield this:

```
<br/>
    He prayeth best who loveth best,
      All things both great and small:
    For the dear God, who loveth us,
      He made and loveth all.
<br/>
    The Marinere, whose eye is bright,
      Whose beard with age is hoar,
    Is gone; and now the wedding-guest
      Turn'd from the bridegroom's door.
<br/>
```

And finally, when the end of the file is discovered, print a couple of end-tags:

```
perl -ne 'if (eof) {print "</body>\n</html>\n"};' rime.txt
```

All this code works together more easily when it's in a file. You'll see that next.

Using a File of Commands with Perl

The following lists *html.pl* which transforms *rime.txt* to HTML using Perl. The numbered callouts in the example guide you through what is happening in the script:

```
#!/usr/bin/perl -p  ❶

if ($. == 1) {  ❷
 chomp($title = $_);
}
print "<!DOCTYPE html>\  ❸
<html xmlns=\"http://www.w3.org/1999/xhtml\">\
```

```
    <head>\
     <title>$title</title>\
     <meta charset=\"utf-8\"/>\
     </head>\
    <body>\
    <h1>$title</h1>\n" if $. == 1;
    s/^(ARGUMENT|I{0,3}V?I{0,2})\.$/<h2>$1<\/h2>/; ❹
    if ($. == 5) { ❺
     s/^([A-Z].*)$/<p>$1<\/p>/;
    }
    if ($. == 9) { ❻
     s/^[ ]*(.*)/  <p>$1<br\/>/;
    }
    if (10..832) { ❼
     s/^([ ]{5,7}.*)/$1<br\/>/;
    }
    if (9..eof) { ❽
     s/^$/<br\/>/;
    }
    if ($. == 833) { ❾
     s/^(.*)$/$1<\/p>\n <\/body>\n<\/html>\n/;
    }
```

❶   This is called the *shebang* directive, which gives a hint to the shell of where the program you are running is located.

❷   If the current line ($.) is line 1, then assign the whole line ($_) to the *$title* variable, chomping off (with chomp) the last character in the string (a newline) in the process.

❸   Print a doctype and several HTML tags at the top of the document at line 1, and reuse the value of the $title variable in several places.

❹   Give the ARGUMENT heading and the Roman numerals *h2* tags.

❺   Surround the introductory paragraph with *p* tags.

❻   Prepend a *p* start-tag to the beginning of the first line of verse, and append a *br* to that line.

❼   Append a *br* tag to the end of each line of verse, except the last line.

❽   Replace each blank line, after line 9, with a *br* tag.

❾   Append *p*, *body*, and *html* end-tags to the last line.

To run this, simply do the following:

```
perl html.pl rime.txt
```

You can also redirect the output with a > to save your output to a file. In the next and final chapter, I'll conclude our regex tutorial.

What You Learned in Chapter 9

- How to use *sed* on the command line
- How to prepend (insert), substitute, and append text (tags) with *sed*
- How to use Perl to do the same

Technical Notes

- AsciiDoc (*http://www.methods.co.nz/asciidoc/*) by Stuart Rackham is a text format that can be converted, using a Python processor, into HTML, PDF, ePUB, DocBook and man pages. The syntax for the text files is similar to Wiki or Markdown and much quicker than hand-coding HTML or XML tags.

- The underscore applies to XML tag names only, not HTML. In addition, XML tags can of course have a much wider range of characters in their names than what is represented in the ASCII set. For more information on characters used in XML names, see *http://www.w3.org/TR/REC-xml/#sec-common-syn*.

- If the command `perldoc` doesn't work, you have some alternatives. First, you can easily read about Perl online at *http://perldoc.perl.org*. (To learn more about $., for example, go to *http://perldoc.perl.org/perlvar.html#Variables-related-to-filehandles*.) If you are on a Mac, try `perldoc5.12`. If you installed Perl from ActiveState, you will find it at `/usr/local/ActivePerl-5.XX/bin`. Both `perl` and `perldoc` are installed at `/usr/local/bin` when compiled and built from source. You can add `/usr/local/bin` to your path so `perl` and `perldoc` will run. For information on setting your path variable, see *http://java.com/en/download/help/path.xml*.

CHAPTER 10

The End of the Beginning

"Unix was not designed to stop you from doing stupid things, because that would also stop you from doing clever things." —Doug Gwyn

Congratulations for making it this far. You're not a regular expression novice anymore. You have been introduced to the most commonly used regular expression syntax. And it will open a lot of possibilities up to you in your work as a programmer.

Learning regular expressions has saved me a lot of time. Let me give you an example.

I use a lot of XSLT at work, and often I have to analyze the tags that exist in a group of XML files.

I showed you part of this in the last chapter, but here is a long one-liner that takes a list of tag names from *lorem.dita* and converts it into a simple XSLT stylesheet:

```
grep -Eo '<[_a-zA-Z][^>]*>' lorem.dita | sort | uniq | sed '1 i\
<xsl:stylesheet version="2.0" xmlns:xsl="http://www.w3.org/1999/XSL/Transform">\

; s/^</\
<xsl:template match="/;s/ id=\".*\"//;s/>$/">\
 <xsl:apply-templates\/>\
<\/xsl:template>/;$ a\
\
</xsl:stylesheet>\
'
```

I know this script may appear a bit acrobatic, but after you work with this stuff for a long time, you start thinking like this. I am not even going to explain what I've done here, because I am sure you can figure it out on your own now.

Here is what the output looks like:

```
<xsl:stylsheet version="2.0" xmlns:xsl="http://www.w3.org/1999/XSL/Transform">
```

```
<xsl:template match="body">
 <xsl:apply-templates/>
</xsl:template>

<xsl:template match="li">
 <xsl:apply-templates/>
</xsl:template>

<xsl:template match="p">
 <xsl:apply-templates/>
</xsl:template>

<xsl:template match="title">
 <xsl:apply-templates/>
</xsl:template>

<xsl:template match="topic">
 <xsl:apply-templates/>
</xsl:template>

<xsl:template match="ul">
 <xsl:apply-templates/>
</xsl:template>

</xsl:stylesheet>
```

That's only a start. Of course, this simple stylesheet will need a lot of editing before it can do anything useful, but this is the kind of thing that can save you a lot of keystrokes.

I'll admit, it would be easier if I put these *sed* commands in a file. As a matter of fact, I did. You'll find *xslt.sed* in the sample archive. This is the file:

```
#!/usr/bin/sed

1 i\
<xsl:stylsheet version="2.0" xmlns:xsl="http://www.w3.org/1999/XSL/Transform">\

s/^</\
<xsl:template match="/;s/ id=\".*\"//;s/>$/">\
 <xsl:apply-templates\/>\
<\/xsl:template>/;$ a\
\
</xsl:stylesheet>\
```

And here is how to run it:

```
grep -Eo '<[_a-zA-Z][^>]*>' lorem.dita | sort | uniq | sed -f xslt.sed
```

Learning More

Even though you have a good strong grip on regex now, there is still lots to learn. I have a couple of suggestions of where to go next.

I pass these recommendations along out of experience and observation, not from any sense of obligation or to be "salesy." I won't get any kickbacks for mentioning them. I talk about them because these resources will actually benefit you.

Jeffrey E. F. Friedl's *Mastering Regular Expressions, Third Edition* is the source many programmers look to for a definitive treatment of the regular expression. Both expansive and well-written, if you are going to do any significant work with regex, you need to have this book on your shelf or in your e-reader. Period.

Jan Goyvaerts and Steven Levithan's *Regular Expressions Cookbook* is another great piece of work, especially if you are comparing different implementations. I'd get this one, too.

The *Regular Expression Pocket Reference: Regular Expressions for Perl, Ruby, PHP, Python, C, Java and .NET* by Tony Stubblebine is a 128-page guide, which, though it is several years old, still remains popular.

Andrew Watt's book *Beginning Regular Expressions* (Wrox, 2005) is highly rated. I have found Bruce Barnett's online *sed* tutorial particularly useful (see *http://www.grymoire.com/Unix/Sed.html*). He demonstrates a number of *sed*'s less understood features, features I have not explained here.

Notable Tools, Implementations, and Libraries

I've mentioned a number of tools, implementations, and libraries in this book. I'll recap those here and mention several others.

Perl

Perl is a popular, general-purpose programming language. A lot of people prefer Perl for text processing with regular expressions over other languages. You likely already have it, but for information on how to install Perl on your system, go to *http://www.perl.org/get.html*. Read about Perl's regular expressions at *http://perldoc.perl.org/perlre.html*. Don't get me wrong. There are plenty of other languages that do a great job with regex, but it pays to have Perl in your toolbox. To learn more, I'd get a copy of the latest edition of Learning Perl (*http://shop.oreilly.com/product/0636920018452.do*), by Randal Schwartz, brian d foy, and Tom Phoenix, also published by O'Reilly.

PCRE

Perl Compatible Regular Expressions or PCRE (see *http://www.pcre.org*) is a regular expression library written in C (both 8-bit and 16-bit). This library mainly consists of functions that may be called within any C framework or from any other language that can use C libraries. It is compatible with Perl 5 regular expressions, as its name suggests, and includes some features from other regex implementations. The Notepad++ editor uses the PCRE library.

pcregrep is an 8-bit, *grep*-like tool that enables you to use the features of the PCRE library on the command line. You used it in Chapter 3. See *http://www.pcre.org* for download information (from *ftp://ftp.csx.cam.ac.uk/pub/software/programming/pcre/*). You can get *pcregrep* for the Mac through Macports (*http://www.macports.org*) by running the command `sudo port install pcre` (Xcode is a prerequisite; see *https://develop er.apple.com/technologies/tools/*, where a login is required). To install it on the Windows platform (binaries), go to *http://gnuwin32.sourceforge.net/packages/pcre.htm*.

Ruby (Oniguruma)

Oniguruma is a regular expression library that is standard with Ruby 1.9; see *http:// oniguruma.rubyforge.org/*. It is written in C and was written specifically to support Ruby. You can try out Ruby's regular expression using Rubular, an online app that supports both 1.8.7 and 1.9.2 (see *http://www.rubular.com* and Figure 10-1). TextMate, by the way, uses the Oniguruma library.

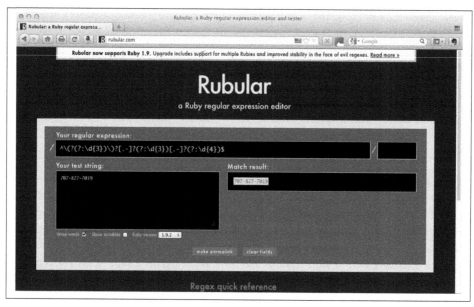

Figure 10-1. Phone number regex in Rubular

Python

Python is a general-purpose programming language that supports regular expressions (see *http://www.python.org*). It was first created by Guido van Rossum in 1991. You can read about Python 3's regular expression syntax here: *http://docs.python.org/py3k/ library/re.html?highlight=regular%20expressions*.

RE2

RE2 is a non-backtracking C++ regular expression library; while RE2 is quite fast, it does not do backtracking or backreferences (see *http://code.google.com/p/re2*). It is available as a CPAN package for Perl and can fall back on Perl's native library if backreferences are needed. For instructions on making API calls, see *http://code.google.com/p/re2/wiki/CplusplusAPI*. For an interesting discussion on RE2, see "Regular Expression Matching in the Wild" at *http://swtch.com/~rsc/regexp/regexp3.html*.

Matching a North American Phone Number

You remember the North American phone number example from the first chapter? You've come a long way since then.

Here is a more robust regular expression for matching phone numbers than the one we used there. It is adapted from Goyvaerts and Levithan's example on page 235 of their *Regular Expressions Cookbook* (first edition):

```
^\(?(?:\d{3})\)?[-.]?(?:\d{3})[-.]?(?:\d{4})$
```

Play with it with the tool of your choice (see it in Reggy in Figure 10-2). By now, you should be able to pick this regex apart with hardly any hand-holding. I'm proud of you for that. But I'll go over it for good measure.

- \^ is the zero-width assertion for the beginning of a line or subject.
- \(? is a literal left parenthesis, but it is optional (?).
- (?:\d{3}) is a non-capturing group matching three consecutive digits.
- \)? is an optional right parenthesis.
- \[-.\]? allows for an optional hyphen or period (dot).
- (?:\d{3}) is another non-capturing group matching three more consecutive digits.
- \[-.\]? allows for an optional hyphen or dot again.
- (?:\d{4}) is yet another non-capturing group matching exactly four consecutive digits.
- $ matches the end of a line or subject.

This expression could be even more refined, but I leave that to you because you can now do it on your own.

Figure 10-2. Phone number regex in Reggy

Matching an Email Address

Lastly, I'll throw one more regular expression at you, an email address:

```
^([\w-.!#$%&;'*+-/=?^_`{|}~]+)@((?:\w+\.)+)(?:[a-zA-Z]{2,4})$
```

This is an adaptation of one provided by Grant Skinner with RegExr. I'd like to challenge you to do your best to explain what each character means in the context of a regular expression, and to see if you can improve on it. I am sure you can.

Thank you for your time. I've enjoyed spending it with you. You should now have a good grasp of the fundamental concepts of regular expressions. You are no longer a member of the beginners' club. I hope you've made friends with regular expressions and learned something worthwhile along the way.

What You Learned in Chapter 10

- How to extract a list of XML elements from a document and convert the list into an XSLT stylesheet.
- Where to find additional resources for learning about regular expressions.
- What are some notable regex tools, implementations, and libraries.
- A slightly, more robust pattern for matching a North American phone number.

Regular Expression Reference

This appendix is a reference for regular expressions.

Regular Expressions in QED

QED (short for Quick Editor) was originally written for the Berkeley Time-Sharing System, which ran on the Scientific Data Systems SDS 940. A rewrite of the original QED editor by Ken Thompson for MIT's Compatible Time-Sharing System yielded one of the earliest (if not the first) practical implementation of regular expressions in computing. Table A-1, taken from pages 3 and 4 of a 1970 Bell Labs memo, outlines the regex features in QED. It amazes me that most of this syntax has remained in use to this day, over 40 years later.

Table A-1. QED regular expressions

Feature	Description
literal	"a) An ordinary character [literal] is a regular expression which matches that character."
^	"b) ^ is a regular expression which matches the null character at the beginning of a line."
$	"c) $ is a regular expression which matches the null character before the character <nl> [newline] (usually at the end of a line)."
.	"d) . is a regular expression which matches any character except <nl> [newline]."
[<string>]	"e) "[<string>]" is a regular expression which matches any of the characters in the <string> and no others."
[^<string>]	"f) "[^<string>] is a regular expression which matches any character but <nl> [newline] and the characters of the <string>."
*	"g) A regular expression followed by "*" is a regular expression which matches any number (including zero) of adjacent occurrences of the text matched by the regular expression."
	"h) Two adjacent regular expressions form a regular expression which matches adjacent occurrences of the text matched by the regular expressions."

Feature	Description
|	"i) Two regular expressions separated by "|" form a regular expression which matches the text matched by either of the regular expressions."
( )	"j) A regular expression in parentheses is a regular expression which matches the same text as the original regular expression. Parentheses are used to alter the order of evaluation implied by g), h), and i): *a(b|c)d* will match *abd* or *acd*, while *ab|cd* matches *ab* or *cd*."
{ }	"k) If "<regexp>" is a regular expression, "{<regexp>}x" is a regular expression, where *x* is any character. This regular expression matches the same things as <regexp>; it has certain side effects as explained under the Substitute command." [The Substitute command was formed *(.,.)S/<regexp>/<string>/* (see page 13 of the memo), similar to the way it is still used in programs like *sed* and Perl.]
\E	"l) If <rexname> is the name of a regular expression named by the E command (below), then "\E<rexname>" is a regular expression which matches the same things as the regular expression specified in the E command. More discussion is presented under the E command." [The \E command allowed you to name a regular expression and repeat its use by name.]
	"m) The null regular expression standing alone is equivalent to the last regular expression encountered. Initially the null regular expression is undefined; it also becomes undefined after an erroneous regular expression and after use of the E command."
	"n) Nothing else is a regular expression."
	"o) No regular expression will match text spread across more than one line."

Metacharacters

There are 14 metacharacters used in regular expressions, each with special meaning, as described in Table A-2. If you want to use one of these characters as a literal, you must precede it with a backslash to escape it. For example, you would escape the dollar sign like this \$, or a backslash like this \\.

Table A-2. Metacharacters in regular expressions

Metacharacter	Name	Code Point	Purpose
.	Full Stop	U+002E	Match any character
\	Backslash	U+005C	Escape a character
|	Vertical Bar	U+007C	Alternation (or)
^	Circumflex	U+005E	Beginning of a line anchor
$	Dollar Sign	U+0024	End of a line anchor
?	Question Mark	U+003F	Zero or one quantifier
*	Asterisk	U+002A	Zero or more quantifier
+	Plus Sign	U+002B	One or more quantifier
[	Left Square Bracket	U+005B	Open character class
]	Right Square Bracket	U+005D	Close character class
{	Left Curly Brace	U+007B	Open quantifier or block
}	Right Curly Brace	007D	Close quantifier or block

Metacharacter	Name	Code Point	Purpose
(	Left Parenthesis	U+0028	Open group
)	Right Parenthesis	U+0029	Close group

Character Shorthands

Table A-3 lists character shorthands used in regular expressions.

Table A-3. Character shorthands

Character Shorthand	Description
\a	Alert
\b	Word boundary
[\b]	Backspace character
\B	Non-word boundary
\cx	Control character
\d	Digit character
\D	Non-digit character
\dxxx	Decimal value for a character
\f	Form feed character
\r	Carriage return
\n	Newline character
\oxxx	Octal value for a character
\s	Space character
\S	Non-space character
\t	Horizontal tab character
\v	Vertical tab character
\w	Word character
\W	Non-word character
\0	Null character
\xxx	Hexadecimal value for a character
\uxxxx	Unicode value for a character

Whitespace

Table A-4 is a list of character shorthands for whitespace.

Table A-4. Whitespace characters

Character Shorthand	Description
\f	Form feed
\h	Horizontal whitespace
\H	Not horizontal whitespace
\n	Newline
\r	Carriage return
\t	Horizontal tab
\v	Vertical whitespace
\V	Not vertical whitespace

Unicode Whitespace Characters

Whitespace characters in Unicode are listed in Table A-5.

Table A-5. Whitespace characters in Unicode

Abbreviation or Nickname	Name	Unicode Code Point	Regex
HT	Horizontal tab	U+0009	\u0009 or \t
LF	Line feed	U+000A	\u000A or \n
VT	Vertical tab	U+000B	\u000B or \v
FF	Form feed	U+000C	\u000C or \f
CR	Carriage return	U+000D	\u000d or \r
SP	Space	U+0020	\u0020 or \s[a]
NEL	Next line	U+0085	\u0085
NBSP	No-break space	U+00A0	\u00A0
—	Ogham space mark	U+1680	\u1680
MVS	Mongolian vowel separator	U+180E	\u180E
BOM	Byte order mark	U+FEFF	\ufeff
NQSP	En quad	U+2000	\u2000
MQSP, Mutton Quad	Em quad	U+2001	\u2001
ENSP, Nut	En space	U+2002	\u2002
EMSP, Mutton	Em space	U+2003	\u2003
3MSP, Thick space	Three-per-em space	U+2004	\u2004
4MSP, Mid space	Four-per-em space	U+2005	\u2005

Abbreviation or Nickname	Name	Unicode Code Point	Regex
6/MSP	Six-per-em space	U+2006	\u2006
FSP	Figure space	U+2007	\u2007
PSP	Punctuation space	U+2008	\u2008
THSP	Thin space	U+2009	\u2009
HSP	Hair space	U+200A	\u200A
ZWSP	Zero width space	U+200B	\u200B
LSEP	Line separator	U+2028	\u2028
PSEP	Paragraph separator	U+2029	\u2029
NNBSP	Narrow no-break space	U+202F	\u202F
MMSP	Medium mathematical space	U+205F	\u205f
IDSP	Ideographic space	U+3000	\u3000

[a] Also matches other whitespace.

Control Characters

Table A-6 shows a way to match control characters in regular expressions.

Table A-6. Matching control characters

Control Character	Unicode Value	Abbreviation	Name
c@[a]	U+0000	NUL	Null
\cA	U+0001	SOH	Start of heading
\cB	U+0002	STX	Start of text
\cC	U+0003	ETX	End of text
\cD	U+0004	EOT	End of transmission
\cE	U+0005	ENQ	Enquiry
\cF	U+0006	ACK	Acknowledge
\cG	U+0007	BEL	Bell
\cH	U+0008	BS	Backspace
\cI	U+0009	HT	Character tabulation or horizontal tab
\cJ	U+000A	LF	Line feed (newline, end of line)
\cK	U+000B	VT	Line tabulation or vertical tab
\cL	U+000C	FF	Form feed
\cM	U+000D	CR	Carriage return
\cN	U+000E	SO	Shift out
\cO	U+000F	SI	Shift in
\cP	U+0010	DLE	Data link escape
\cQ	U+0011	DC1	Device control one

Control Character	Unicode Value	Abbreviation	Name
\cR	U+0012	DC2	Device control two
\cS	U+0013	DC3	Device control three
\cT	U+0014	DC4	Device control four
\cU	U+0015	NAK	Negative acknowledge
\cV	U+0016	SYN	Synchronous idle
\cW	U+0017	ETB	End of Transmission block
\cX	U+0018	CAN	Cancel
\cY	U+0019	EM	End of medium
\cZ	U+001A	SUB	Substitute
\c[	U+001B	ESC	Escape
\c\	U+001C	FS	Information separator four
\c]	U+001D	GS	Information separator three
\c^	U+001E	RS	Information separator two
\c_	U+001F	US	Information separator one

a Can use upper- or lowercase. For example, \cA or \ca are equivalent; however, Java implementations require uppercase.

Character Properties

Table A-7 lists character property names for use with \p{*property*} or \P{*property*}.

Table A-7. Character properties^a

Property	Description
C	Other
Cc	Control
Cf	Format
Cn	Unassigned
Co	Private use
Cs	Surrogate
L	Letter
Ll	Lowercase letter
Lm	Modifier letter
Lo	Other letter
Lt	Title case letter
Lu	Uppercase letter
L&	Ll, Lu, or Lt
M	Mark
Mc	Spacing mark

Property	Description
Me	Enclosing mark
Mn	Non-spacing mark
N	Number
Nd	Decimal number
Nl	Letter number
No	Other number
P	Punctuation
Pc	Connector punctuation
Pd	Dash punctuation
Pe	Close punctuation
Pf	Final punctuation
Pi	Initial punctuation
Po	Other punctuation
Ps	Open punctuation
S	Symbol
Sc	Currency symbol
Sk	Modifier symbol
Sm	Mathematical symbol
So	Other symbol
Z	Separator
Zl	Line separator
Zp	Paragraph separator
Zs	Space separator

[a] See pcresyntax(3) at *http://www.pcre.org/pcre.txt*.

Script Names for Character Properties

Table A-8 shows the language script names for use with /p{*property*} or /P{*property*}.

Table A-8. Script names[a]

Arabic (Arab)	Glagolitic (Glag)	Lepcha (Lepc)	Samaritan (Samr)
Armenian (Armn)	Gothic (Goth)	Limbu (Limb)	Saurashtra (Saur)
Avestan (Avst)	Greek (Grek)	Linear B (Linb)	Shavian (Shaw)
Balinese (Bali)	Gujarati (Gujr)	Lisu (Lisu)	Sinhala (Sinh)
Bamum (Bamu)	Gurmukhi (Guru)	Lycian (Lyci)	Sundanese (Sund)
Bengali (Beng)	Han (Hani)	Lydian (Lydi)	Syloti Nagri (Sylo)
Bopomofo (Bopo)	Hangul (Hang)	Malayalam (Mlym)	Syriac (Syrc)

Braille (Brai) Hanunoo (Hano) Meetei Mayek (Mtei) Tagalog (Tglg)

Buginese (Bugi) Hebrew (Hebr) Mongolian (Mong) Tagbanwa (Tagb)

Buhid (Buhd) Hiragana (Hira) Myanmar (Mymr) Tai Le (Tale)

Canadian Aboriginal (Cans) Hrkt: Katakana or Hiragana) New Tai Lue (Talu) Tai Tham (Lana)

Carian (Cari) Imperial Aramaic (Armi) Nko (Nkoo) Tai Viet (Tavt)

Cham (None) Inherited (Zinh/Qaai) Ogham (Ogam) Tamil (Taml)

Cherokee (Cher) Inscriptional Pahlavi (Phli) Ol Chiki (Olck) Telugu (Telu)

Common (Zyyy) Inscriptional Parthian (Prti) Old Italic (Ital) Thaana (Thaa)

Coptic (Copt/Qaac) Javanese (Java) Old Persian (Xpeo) Thai (None)

Cuneiform (Xsux) Kaithi (Kthi) Old South Arabian (Sarb) Tibetan (Tibt)

Cypriot (Cprt) Kannada (Knda) Old Turkic (Orkh) Tifinagh (Tfng)

Cyrillic (Cyrl) Katakana (Kana) Oriya (Orya) Ugaritic (Ugar)

Deseret (Dsrt) Kayah Li (Kali) Osmanya (Osma) Unknown (Zzzz)

Devanagari (Deva) Kharoshthi (Khar) Phags Pa (Phag) Vai (Vaii)

Egyptian Hieroglyphs (Egyp) Khmer (Khmr) Phoenician (Phnx) Yi (Yiii)

Ethiopic (Ethi) Lao (Laoo) Rejang (Rjng)

Georgian (Geor) Latin (Latn) Runic (Runr)

[a] See pcresyntax(3) at *http://www.pcre.org/pcre.txt* or *http://ruby.runpaint.org/regexps#properties*.

POSIX Character Classes

Table A-9 shows a list of POSIX character classes.

Table A-9. POSIX character classes

Character Class	Description
[[:alnum:]]	Alphanumeric characters (letters and digits)
[[:alpha:]]	Alphabetic characters (letters)
[[:ascii:]]	ASCII characters (all 128)
[[:blank:]]	Blank characters
[[:ctrl:]]	Control characters
[[:digit:]]	Digits
[[:graph:]]	Graphic characters
[[:lower:]]	Lowercase letters
[[:print:]]	Printable characters
[[:punct:]]	Punctuation characters
[[:space:]]	Whitespace characters
[[:upper:]]	Uppercase letters
[[:word:]]	Word characters

Character Class	Description
[[:xdigit:]]	Hexadecimal digits

Options/Modifiers

Table A-10 and Table A-11 list options and modifiers.

Table A-10. Options in regular expressions

Option	Description	Supported by
(?d)	Unix lines	Java
(?i)	Case insensitive	PCRE, Perl, Java
(?J)	Allow duplicate names	PCRE[a]
(?m)	Multiline	PCRE, Perl, Java
(?s)	Single line (dotall)	PCRE, Perl, Java
(?u)	Unicode case	Java
(?U)	Default match lazy	PCRE
(?x)	Ignore whitespace, comments	PCRE, Perl, Java
(?-...)	Unset or turn off options	PCRE

[a] See "Named Subpatterns" in *http://www.pcre.org/pcre.txt*.

Table A-11. Perl modifiers (flags)[a]

Modifier	Description
a	Match \d, \s, \w and POSIX in ASCII range only
c	Keep current position after match fails
d	Use default, native rules of the platform
g	Global matching
i	Case-insensitive matching
l	Use current locale's rules
m	Multiline strings
p	Preserve the matched string
s	Treat strings as a single line
u	Use Unicode rules when matching
x	Ignore whitespace and comments

[a] See *http://perldoc.perl.org/perlre.html#Modifiers*.

ASCII Code Chart with Regex

Table A-12 is an ASCII code chart with regex cross-references.

Table A-12. ASCII code chart

Binary	Oct	Dec	Hex	Char	Kybd	Regex	Name
00000000	0	0	0	NUL	^@	\c@	Null character
00000001	1	1	1	SOH	^A	\cA	Start of header
00000010	2	2	2	STX	^B	\cB	Start of text
00000011	3	3	3	ETX	^C	\cC	End of text
00000100	4	4	4	EOT	^D	\cD	End of transmission
00000101	5	5	5	ENQ	^E	\cE	Enquiry
00000110	6	6	6	ACK	^F	\cF	Acknowledgment
00000111	7	7	7	BEL	^G	\a, \cG	Bell
00001000	10	8	8	BS	^H	[\b], \cH	Backspace
00001001	11	9	9	HT	^I	\t, \cI	Horizontal tab
00001010	12	10	0A	LF	^J	\n, \cJ	Line feed
00001011	13	11	0B	VT	^K	\v, \cK	Vertical tab
00001100	14	12	0C	FF	^L	\f, \cL	Form feed
00001101	15	13	0D	CR	^M	\r, \cM	Carriage return
00001110	16	14	0E	SO	^N	\cN	Shift out
00001111	17	15	0F	SI	^O	\cO	Shift in
00010000	20	16	10	DLE	^P	\cP	Data link escape
00010001	21	17	11	DC1	^Q	\cQ	Device control 1 (XON)
00010010	22	18	12	DC2	^R	\cR	Device control 2
00010011	23	19	13	DC3	^S	\cS	Device control 3 (XOFF)
00010100	24	20	14	DC4	^T	\cT	Device control 4
00010101	25	21	15	NAK	^U	\cU	Negative acknowledgement
00010110	26	22	16	SYN	^V	\cV	Synchronous idle
00010111	27	23	17	ETB	^W	\cW	End of transmission block
00011000	30	24	18	CAN	^X	\cX	Cancel
00011001	31	25	19	EM	^Y	\cY	End of medium
00011010	32	26	1A	SUB	^Z	\cZ	Substitute
00011011	33	27	1B	ESC	^[	\e, \c[	Escape
00011100	34	28	1C	FS	^\	\c\	File separator
00011101	35	29	1D	GS	^]	\c]	Group separator
00011110	36	30	1E	RS	^^	\c^	Record separator
00011111	37	31	1F	US	^_	\c_	Unit Separator
00100000	40	32	20	SP	SP	\s, [ ]	Space
00100001	41	33	21	!	!	!	Exclamation mark
00100010	42	34	22	"	"	"	Quotation mark

Binary	Oct	Dec	Hex	Char	Kybd	Regex	Name
00100011	43	35	23	#	#	#	Number sign
00100100	44	36	24	$	$	\$	Dollar sign
00100101	45	37	25	%	%	%	Percent sign
00100110	46	38	26	&	&	&	Ampersand
00100111	47	39	27	'	'	'	Apostrophe
00101000	50	40	28	(	(	(, \(	Left parenthesis
00101001	51	41	29	)	)	), \)	Right parenthesis
00101010	52	42	2A	*	*	*	Asterisk
00101011	53	43	2B	+	+	+	Plus sign
00101100	54	44	2C	"	"	"	Comma
00101101	55	45	2D	-	-	-	Hyphen-minus
00101110	56	46	2E	.	.	\., [.]	Full stop
00101111	57	47	2F	/	/	/	Solidus
00110000	60	48	30	0	0	\d, [0]	Digit zero
00110001	61	49	31	1	1	\d, [1]	Digit one
00110010	62	50	32	2	2	\d, [2]	Digit two
00110011	63	51	33	3	3	\d, [3]	Digit three
00110100	64	52	34	4	4	\d, [4]	Digit four
00110101	65	53	35	5	5	\d, [5]	Digit five
00110110	66	54	36	6	6	\d, [6]	Digit six
00110111	67	55	37	7	7	\d, [7]	Digit seven
00111000	70	56	38	8	8	\d, [8]	Digit eight
00111001	71	57	39	9	9	\d, [9]	Digit nine
00111010	72	58	3A	:	:	:	Colon
00111011	73	59	3B	;	;	;	Semicolon
00111100	74	60	3C	<	<	<	Less-than sign
00111101	75	61	3D	=	=	=	Equals sign
00111110	76	62	3E	>	>	>	Greater-than sign
00111111	77	63	3F	?	?	?	Question mark
01000000	100	64	40	@	@	@	Commercial at
01000001	101	65	41	A	A	\w, [A]	Latin capital letter A
01000010	102	66	42	B	B	\w, [B]	Latin capital letter B
01000011	103	67	43	C	C	\w, [C]	Latin capital letter C
01000100	104	68	44	D	D	\w, [D]	Latin capital letter D
01000101	105	69	45	E	E	\w, [E]	Latin capital letter E
01000110	106	70	46	F	F	\w, [F]	Latin capital letter F

Binary	Oct	Dec	Hex	Char	Kybd	Regex	Name
01000111	107	71	47	G	G	\w, [G]	Latin capital letter G
01001000	110	72	48	H	H	\w, [H]	Latin capital letter H
01001001	111	73	49	I	I	\w, [I]	Latin capital letter I
01001010	112	74	4A	J	J	\w, [J]	Latin capital letter J
01001011	113	75	4B	K	K	\w, [K]	Latin capital letter K
01001100	114	76	4C	L	L	\w, [L]	Latin capital letter L
01001101	115	77	4D	M	M	\w, [M]	Latin capital letter M
01001110	116	78	4E	N	N	\w, [N]	Latin capital letter N
01001111	117	79	4F	O	O	\w, [O]	Latin capital letter O
01010000	120	80	50	P	P	\w, [P]	Latin capital letter P
01010001	121	81	51	Q	Q	\w, [Q]	Latin capital letter Q
01010010	122	82	52	R	R	\w, [R]	Latin capital letter R
01010011	123	83	53	S	S	\w, [S]	Latin capital letter S
01010100	124	84	54	T	T	\w, [T]	Latin capital letter T
01010101	125	85	55	U	U	\w, [U]	Latin capital letter U
01010110	126	86	56	V	V	\w, [V]	Latin capital letter V
01010111	127	87	57	W	W	\w, [W]	Latin capital letter W
01011000	130	88	58	X	X	\w, [X]	Latin capital letter X
01011001	131	89	59	Y	Y	\w, [Y]	Latin capital letter Y
01011010	132	90	5A	Z	Z	\w, [Z]	Latin capital letter Z
01011011	133	91	5B	[	[	\[	Left square bracket
01011100	134	92	5C	\	\	\	Reverse solidus
01011101	135	93	5D	]	]	\]	Right square bracket
01011110	136	94	5E	^	^	^, [^]	Circumflex accent
01011111	137	95	5F	_	_	_, [_]	Low line
00100000	140	96	60	`	`	\`	Grave accent
01100001	141	97	61	a	a	\w, [a]	Latin small letter A
01100010	142	98	62	b	b	\w, [b]	Latin small letter B
01100011	143	99	63	c	c	\w, [c]	Latin small letter C
01100100	144	100	64	d	d	\w, [d]	Latin small letter D
01100101	145	101	65	e	e	\w, [e]	Latin small letter E
01100110	146	102	66	f	f	\w, [f]	Latin small letter F
01100111	147	103	67	g	g	\w, [g]	Latin small letter G
01101000	150	104	68	h	h	\w, [h]	Latin small letter H
01101001	151	105	69	i	i	\w, [i]	Latin small letter I
01101010	152	106	6A	j	j	\w, [j]	Latin small letter J

Binary	Oct	Dec	Hex	Char	Kybd	Regex	Name
01101011	153	107	6B	k	k	\w, [k]	Latin small letter K
01101100	154	108	6C	l	l	\w, [l]	Latin small letter L
01101101	155	109	6D	m	m	\w, [m]	Latin small letter M
01101110	156	110	6E	n	n	\w, [n]	Latin small letter N
01101111	157	111	6F	o	o	\w, [o]	Latin small letter O
01110000	160	112	70	p	p	\w, [p]	Latin small letter P
01110001	161	113	71	q	q	\w, [q]	Latin small letter Q
01110010	162	114	72	r	r	\w, [r]	Latin small letter R
01110011	163	115	73	s	s	\w, [s]	Latin small letter S
01110100	164	116	74	t	t	\w, [t]	Latin small letter T
01110101	165	117	75	u	u	\w, [u]	Latin small letter U
01110110	166	118	76	v	v	\w, [v]	Latin small letter V
01110111	167	119	77	w	w	\w, [w]	Latin small letter W
01111000	170	120	78	x	x	\w, [x]	Latin small letter X
01111001	171	121	79	y	y	\w, [y]	Latin small letter Y
01111010	172	122	7A	z	z	\w, [z]	Latin small letter Z
01111011	173	123	7B	{	{	{	Left curly brace
01111100	174	124	7C	|	|	|	Vertical line (Bar)
01111101	175	125	7D	}	}	}	Right curly brace
01111110	176	126	7E	~	~	\~	Tilde
01111111	177	127	7F	DEL	^?	\c?	Delete

Technical Notes

You can find Ken Thompson and Dennis Ritchie's QED memo-cum manual at *http://cm.bell-labs.com/cm/cs/who/dmr/qedman.pdf*.

Regular Expression Glossary

anchor

Specifies a location in a line or string. For example, the caret or circumflex character (^) signifies the beginning of a line or string of characters, and the dollar sign character ($), the end of a line or string.

alternation

Separating a list of regular expressions with a vertical bar (|) character, indicating *or*. In other words, match any of the regular expressions separated by one or more | characters. In some applications, such as *grep* or *sed* that use basic regular expressions (BREs), the | is preceded by a backslash, as in \|. *See also* basic regular expressions.

ASCII

American Standard Code for Information Interchange. A 128-character encoding scheme for English (Latin) characters developed in the 1960s. *See also* Unicode.

assertions

See zero-width assertions.

atom

See metacharacter.

atomic group

A grouping that turns off backtracking when a regular expression inside (?>...) fails to match. *See also* backtracking, groups.

backreference

Refers to a previous regular expression captured with parentheses using a reference in the form of \1, \2, and so forth.

backtracking

Stepping back, character by character, through an attempted match to find a successful match. Used with a greedy match, but not a lazy or possessive match. Catastrophic backtracking occurs when a regex processor makes perhaps thousands of attempts to make a match and consumes a vast amount (read *most*) of the computing resources available. One way to avoid catastrophic backtracking is with atomic grouping. *See also* atomic group, greedy match, lazy match, possessive match.

basic regular expressions

An early implementation of regular expressions that is less advanced and considered obsolete by most. Also called *BREs*. BREs required you to escape certain characters in order for them to function as metacharacters, such as braces (\{ and }\). *See also* extended regular expressions.

bound

See quantifier.

bracketed expression

A regular expression given in square brackets; for example, *[a-f]*, that is, the range of lowercase letters a through f. *See also* character class.

branch

A concatenation of pieces in a regular expression in POSIX.1 terminology. *See also* POSIX.

BREs

See basic regular expressions.

capturing group

See groups.

catastrophic backtracking

See backtracking.

character class

Usually, a set of characters enclosed in square brackets; for example, *[a-bA-B0-9]* is a character class for all upper- and lowercase characters plus digits in the ASCII or Low Basic Latin character set.

character escape

A character preceded by a backward slash. Examples are \t (horizontal tab), \v (vertical tab), and \f (form feed).

character set

See character class.

code point

See Unicode.

composability

"A schema language (or indeed a programming language) provides a number of atomic objects and a number of methods of composition. The methods of composition can be used to combine atomic objects into compound objects which can in turn be composed into further compound objects. The composability of the language is the degree to which the various methods of composition can be applied uniformly to all the various objects of the language, both atomic and compound…Composability improves ease of learning and ease of use. Composability also tends to improve the ratio between complexity and power: for a given amount of complexity, a more composable language will be more powerful than a less composable one." From James Clark, "The Design of RELAX NG," *http://www.thaiopensource.com/relaxng/design.html#section:5*.

ed

The Unix line editor created by Ken Thompson in 1971, which implemented regular expressions. It was a precursor to *sed* and *vi*.

EREs

See extended regular expressions.

extended regular expressions

Extended regular expressions or EREs added additional functionality to basic regular expressions or BREs, such as alternation (\|) and quantifiers such as ? and +, which work with *egrep* (extended grep). These new features were delineated in IEEE POSIX standard 1003.2-1992. You can use the *-E* option with *grep* (same as using *egrep*), which means that you want to use extended regular expressions rather than basic regular expressions. *See also* alternation, basic regular expressions, grep.

flag

See modifier.

greedy match

A greedy match consumes as much of a target string as possible, and then backtracks through the string to attempt to find a match. *See* backtracking, lazy match, possessive match.

grep

A Unix command-line utility for searching strings with regular expressions. Invented by Ken Thompson in 1973, *grep* is said to have grown out of the *ed* editor command g/re/p (global/regular expression/print). Superseded but not retired by *egrep* (or *grep -E*—which has additional metacharacters such as |, +, ?, (, and)—*grep* uses basic regular expressions, whereas *grep -E* or *egrep* use extended regular expressions.

fgrep (*grep -F*) searches files using literal strings and metacharacters like $, *, and | don't have special meaning. *See also* basic regular expressions, extended regular expressions.

groups

Groups combine regular expression atoms within a pair of parentheses, ( ). In some applications, such as *grep* or *sed* (without the *-E*), you must precede the parenthesis with a backslash, as in \) or \(. There are capturing groups and non-capturing groups. A capturing group stores the captured group in memory so that it can be reused while a non-capturing group does not. Atomic groups do not backtrack. *See also* atomic group.

hexadecimal

A base 16 numbering system represented by the digits 0–9 and the letters A–F or a–f. For example, the base 10 number 15 is represented as F in hexadecimal, and 16 is 10.

hold buffer

See hold space.

hold space

Used by *sed* to store one or more lines for further processing. Also called the *hold buffer*. *See also* pattern space, *sed*.

lazy match

A lazy match consumes a subject string one character at a time, attempting to find a match. It does not backtrack. *See also* backtracking, greedy match, possessive match.

literal

See string literal.

lookaround

See lookahead, lookbehind.

lookahead

A regular expression that matches only if another specified regular expression follows the first. A positive lookahead uses the syntax `regex(?=regex)`. A negative look-

ahead means that the regular expression is *not* followed by a regular expression that follows the first. Uses the syntax `regex(?! regex)`.

lookbehind

A regular expression that matches only if another specified regular expression precedes the first. A positive lookbehind uses the syntax `regex(?<=regex)`. A negative lookbehind means that the regular expression is *not* followed by a regular expression that precedes the first. Uses the syntax `regex(?<!regex)`.

matching

A regular expression may match a given pattern in text and then, depending on the application, trigger a result.

metacharacter

A character that has a special meaning in regular expressions. These characters are (the commas in this list are separators) ., \, \|, *, +, ?, ~, $, [,], (,), {, }. Metacharacters are also called *atoms*.

modifier

A character placed after a match or substitution pattern that modifies the matching process. For example, the *i* modifier makes the match case-insensitive. Also called a *flag*.

negation

Indicates that a regular expression does not match a given pattern. Given inside character classes with a leading caret character, as in `[^2-7]`, which would match other digits besides 2, 3, 4, 5, 6 and 7—that is, 0, 1, 8, 9.

negative lookahead

See lookahead.

negative lookbehind

See lookbehind.

non-capturing group

A group within parentheses that is not captured (that is, stored in memory for future use). The syntax for a non-capturing group is *(?:pattern)*. *See also* groups.

octal characters

A character may be represented with an octal notation in regular expressions. In regular expressions, a character given in octal form is specified as \o*xx* where the *x* represents a number in the range 1–9, using one to two places. For example, \o represents the character *é*, the Latin small letter *e* with an acute accent.

occurrence constraint

See quantifier.

options

Allows you to turn on and off options that modify the match. For example, the (?i) option indicates that the match will be case-insensitive. Similar to modifiers, but they use a different syntax. *See also* modifier.

pattern space

The *sed* program normally processes as input one line at a time. As each line is processed, it is placed in what is called *pattern space*, to which patterns may be applied. This is also called the *work buffer*. *See also* hold space, sed.

Perl

A general-purpose programming language created by Larry Wall in 1987, Perl is known for its strong support of regular expressions and its text processing capabilities. See *http://www.perl.org*.

piece

A portion of a regular expression, usually concatenated, in POSIX.1 terminology. *See also* POSIX.

positive lookahead

See lookahead.

positive lookbehind

See lookbehind.

POSIX

Portable Operating System Interface for Unix. A family of Unix-related standards by the Institute of Electrical and Electronics

Engineers (IEEE). The most recent POSIX standard for regular expressions is POSIX.1-2008 (see *http://standards.ieee.org/findstds/standard/1003.1-2008.html*).

possessive match

A possessive match consumes an entire subject string in one fell swoop, attempting to find a match. It does not backtrack. *See also* backtracking, greedy match, lazy match.

quantifier

Defines the number of times a regular expression may occur in an attempted match. An integer or pair of integers separated by a comma, surrounded by braces, is one form; for example, {3} indicates that the expression may occur exactly three times (with older tools that use basic regular expressions, you must escape the braces, as in \{3\}).

Other quantifiers include ? (zero or one times), + (one or more), and * (zero or more). A quantifier is also called a *bound* or a *modifier*. By themselves, quantifiers are greedy. There are also lazy quantifiers (e.g., {3}?) and possessive quantifiers (e.g., {3}+). *See also* basic regular expressions, greedy match, lazy match, possessive match.

regular expression

A specially encoded string of characters that, when used within an application or utility, may match other strings or sets of strings. First described in the early 1950s by the mathematician Stephen Kleene (1909–1994) in his work with formal language theory in his book *Introduction to Metamathematics*, published in 1952. Began to gain momentum in computer science with the work of Ken Thompson, *et al.* on the QED editor (under the General Electric Time Sharing System [GE-TSS] on a GE-635 computer) and, later, other tools under AT&T Bell Labs' Unix operating system in the early 1970s.

sed

A Unix streaming editor that accepts regular expressions and transforms text. It was developed in the early 1970s by Lee McMahon at Bell Labs. Here is an example of *sed*: `sed -n 's/this/that/g\' file.ext > new.ext`. Use *sed -E* to indicate that you want to use extended regular expressions. *See also* extended regular expressions.

string literal

A string of characters interpreted literally—for example, the literal string "It is an ancyent Marinere" as opposed to something like "[Ii]t[ ]is[ ].*nere."

Unicode

Unicode is a system for encoding characters for writing systems of the world. Each character in Unicode is assigned a numeric code point. There are over 100,000 characters represented in Unicode. In regular expressions, a Unicode character can be specified as \u*xxxx* or \x*{xxxx}*, where *x* represents a hexadecimal number in the range 0–9, A–F (or a–f), using one to four places. For example, \u00E9 represents the character *é*, the Latin small letter *e* with an acute accent. *See also http://www.unicode.org*.

vi

A Unix editor that was first developed in 1976 by Bill Joy and that uses regular expressions. The *vim* editor is an improved replacement for *vi*, developed primarily by Bram Moolenaar (see *http://www.vim.org*). I currently use six or seven different editors during a regular work day, but the one I use most often is *vim*. In fact, if I were shipwrecked on a desert island, and could have only one text editor, I would choose *vim*. No question.

vim

See vi.

work buffer

See pattern space.

zero-width assertions

Boundaries that do not consume any characters in a match. ^ and $, which match the beginning and end of a line, respectively, are examples.

Index

We'd like to hear your suggestions for improving our indexes. Send email to index@oreilly.com.

About the Author

Michael Fitzgerald, a programmer and consultant, has written 10 technical books for O'Reilly and John Wiley & Sons, as well as several articles for the O'Reilly Network. He was a member of the original committee that created the RELAX NG schema language for XML.

Colophon

The animal on the cover of *Introducing Regular Expressions* is a fruit bat.

Members of the suborder *Megachiroptera* and family *Pteropodidae* are known as fruit bats, flying foxes, old world fruit bats, or megabats. Despite the latter nickname, members of the Pteropodidae family vary greatly in size—the smallest measure six centimeters, while others weigh in at two pounds, with wingspans up to approximately five feet long.

True to their name, fruit bats are frugivorous, or nectavorious, meaning they eat fruit or lick nectar from flowers. Some use their teeth to bite through fruit skin and actually eat the fruit, while others lick juices from crushed fruit. Because many of them dine on flower nectar, fruit bats are excellent pollinators and seed-spreaders—in fact, the World Bat Sanctuary estimates that approximately 95% of all new rainforest growth can be attributed to fruit bats' distribution of seeds. This relationship between the bats and plants is a form of mutualism—the way organisms of different species interact biologically for a mutual fitness benefit—known as chiropterophily.

Fruit bats can be found all over the world, though they prefer warm, tropical climates, due in part to the availability of fruit and flowers. While they're excellent flyers, fruit bats are known for their clumsy landings; they often crash land into trees or try to grab limbs with their feet in order to stop themselves. This perpetuates the misconception that they're blind, when in fact, fruit bats are said to have the best vision of all the bat species, most of which rely on echolocation to get around. Fruit bats use vision—along with their advanced senses of smell—to locate food and navigate.

The cover image is from Cassell's *Natural History*. The cover font is Adobe ITC Garamond. The text font is Linotype Birka; the heading font is Adobe Myriad Condensed; and the code font is LucasFont's TheSansMonoCondensed.